RELIGIOUS MYSTERIES
OF THE ORIENT

The Sacred Picture of Caodai.

THE SACRED PICTURE OF CAODAI *showing tolerance and love of the good in all religions. Grouped beneath the All-Seeing Eye of God stand the Masters: Christ, Buddha, Mohammed, Confucius, Lao-Tze, and Quan Yin.*

Standing with Them on the Holy Altar are two saints of Caodai, and the holy artifacts; the Sacred Lamp of the Eternal Flame, symbolizing the Universal Monad (Divine Soul), the two candles representative of the two aspects of the Monad—the male and female Logos, *the bowl of fruit illustrative of the* Yin *(female* Logos) *and the vase of flowers the* Yang *(male* Logos), *the cup of tea and the cup of water again representing the female and male* Logos, *and the three glasses of wine symbolizing the spiritual being and vital energy.*

These offerings of flowers, wine and tea, respectively, symbolize the three constitutive elements of the human being, called by the Caodaists the Tinh, *the* Khi, *and the* Than. *The* Tinh *is the essence of all matter; the cosmic sperm from which comes forth all life. The* Khi *is the essence of breath, health, and vitality. The* Than *is the essence of the intelligence principle, double in man: the superior mental is divine spirit (mind), and the inferior mental the intellect (brain).*

The Altar of Caodai sits with the Divine Eye of God installed to the north, the symbols of male Logos *and* Yang *on the left and the female* Logos *and* Yin *on the right, representative of the universal truth of the dual principle of Yang and Yin that form the origin of all creation.*

Ron Ormond and Ormond McGill.

This picture, after half a century of veneration, was taken from the shrine and presented to Ron Ormond and myself by the three cardinals, Nguyen-Trung-Hau, Le-Thien-Phuoc, and Thuong-Van-Trang, Conservatory of Caodaism, Tayninh, Vietnam. As it is representative of our journey into the unknown to search out strange religious practices of the Orient, it is used as an appropriate frontispiece to this book.

RELIGIOUS MYSTERIES OF THE ORIENT

Ormond McGill
and
Ron Ormond

Photography by Ron Ormond

South Brunswick and New York: A. S. Barnes and Company
London: Thomas Yoseloff Ltd

A. S. Barnes and Co., Inc.
Cranbury, New Jersey 08512

Thomas Yoseloff Ltd
108 New Bond Street
London W1Y OQX, England

Library of Congress Cataloging in Publication Data

McGill, Ormond.
    Religious mysteries of the Orient.

    Includes index.
    1. East (Far East) —Religion. 2. Asia, Southeastern—Religion.
3. India—Religion. I. Ormond, Ron, joint author. II. Title.
BL1055.M29   299'.5   73-22596
ISBN 0-498-01496-7

PRINTED IN THE UNITED STATES OF AMERICA

Contents

Acknowledgments

Special thanks to my partner and co-author, Ron Ormond, who shared the journey with me exploring these great religious mysteries of the Orient, and whose talents for reporting and photography were used so searchingly. And to the many friends, from a variety of lands, who helped us along the way, viz.:

In the United States, Ralph S. Willard, Ph.D., Joyce Newton, Jack Lewis, William Panneck, Lester Kashiwa, M.D., and Paul Fujimoto. *In the Philippine Islands,* Jose K. Lapus, Jose Dayrit, Guillesmo Tolentino, and Joseph Navarro. *In Hong Kong,* Ng Siu Chor, Thomas Tam, David Yew, and Ernest Lamp. *In Taiwan,* Dr. Hsu, Guruni Siu Ho Yang, P. T. Chen, and John Wu. *In Vietnam,* Nguyen-Thung-Hau, Le-Thied-Phoc, Thruong-Van-Trang, and Phan-Tai-Doam. *In Thailand,* Harold M. Young, Guruni Varamai, and Siva Namasondhi. *In Burma,* U Thoung Pe and U. Chittee. *In India,* Sadhu Parimal Bandu, G. Kumar, H. M. Vakil, P. Ghosh, Basil Rodriges, Antique Anver.

ORMOND MCGILL
Your Escort On The Journey

Introduction

The adventures reported in these pages are true; they were personally lived and experienced by my partner, Ron Ormond, and myself during a journey into the Far East to film a motion picture documentary of the great religious mysteries of the Orient. On our return, we lectured and privately printed some of our notes and photographs under the title *Into The Strange Unknown*. The response was electric, as many of the incidents had a mysterious, metaphysical overtone. Some of the adventures are fantastic, and assuredly prove that *truth is stranger than fiction*. We have written of these adventures in this book.

But, this is far more than a book of adventures, as underneath the adventures will be found the endless seeking of man for answers to his questions about the unknown, religion, and the true nature of the self. To these questions we found some most penetrating oriental answers, uniquely crystallized as our minds of the West met minds of the East.

First, perhaps, I should write briefly about ourselves.

Ron is a motion picture producer, a thoroughly qualified man in all aspects of the field. I am a magician and hypnotist by profession, and an amateur naturalist. We have been friends for years, and are of that temperament that tries to seek out things bordering on the offbeat. Further, we both have an interest in religion (in the broadest sense), including occultism. Thus, we planned our journey into the unknown.

Little did we realize what amazing experiences lay before us, or how striking would be the impact of our adventures on our personal lives. We truthfully feel we have probed what many consider "unanswerables" about God, man, life and death, and the hereafter, as seen through the eyes of most devout people of the Far East. I present our findings in this book.

Col. Ron Ormond and the late Cecil B. DeMille discuss the filming of Great Religious Mysteries of the Orient.

As an introduction, picture us as our Air India's big four-engined Viscount touched "wheels down" at Dum-Dum airport in Calcutta. We heaved a sigh of relief. At long last we were in the very heart of "the land of magic." Seven months of breathtaking adventures lay behind us, adventures that had brought our cameras to places seldom seen by white men's eyes.

In the Philippines, we had observed and participated in "Oriental Christianity." Here we had seen the miraculous cures of The Black Jesus at the famed Quiapo, and the almost cruel practices of devotion by The Flagellantes. Here, also, we had photographed Terte, the remarkable faith healer of San Fabian, the man we have chosen to call (for want of a better name) "the fourth-dimensional surgeon," as he seemingly performs bloodless operations without use of scalpel.

Long climbs up stone steps lead to the remote monasteries on the lonely hilltops.

Interiors of the monasteries, temples, and oriental religious shrines are utterly fantastic.

Taoist temples in the Republic of China.

Introduction

In Hong Kong, we were given entree to another spectacle seldom watched by the occidental, The Spirit Festival of Cheung Chau Junkers, where, for three momentous days and nights, thousands of Chinese prayed for their departed and offered lavish food and mountains of bread to the spirits.

In Taiwan, we participated in the divining methods of The Red Swastika Society, as they called upon the spirits of ancient gurus to prophesy.

I could go on and tell you about adventures among the aboriginal tribes that roam the mountain regions of the little-explored portions of the Orient. Some to this day worship evil forces, while others practice with great skill the art of headhunting. And I could tell you of our spending days and nights in mysterious Buddhist monasteries perched on remote hilltops. Many of these adventures I will recount in this book.

For a start, let me tell of our experiences with The Red Swastika Society. To preface this, I should say that the name of this society may be misleading, as The Red Swastika Society is neither red in the sense of being communistic nor Nazi in its use of the swastika as its symbol. This is entirely a religious organization, the red of its name standing for the life-giving blood of mankind, the swastika used as the ancient symbol of divinity, God, creation, or truth. It is the true swastika, you will notice,[1] not the reversed swastika as used by Hitler in World War Two.

The Taiwanese newspapers devoted considerable space to our unique quest for filming unusual religious practices in the Orient. After such press notices, a number of phone calls were forthcoming, but the one that proved most interesting was from a Dr. Hsu.

Most oriental organizations of a religious nature are based on the teachings of Buddha, Lao-Tze, or Confucius, but Dr. Hsu's organization, "The Red Swastika Society," while accepting aspects of all three of these, had features distinctly its own.

The Society was founded in China many years ago, and since the communist takeover of the Mainland has migrated to quarters in Hong Kong and Taiwan. Among their venerated treasures is a revelation of the word of God said to have been given the Chinese at the same time that Moses was given The Ten Commandments on Mount Sinai. This revered text, preserved through the centuries in twelve chapters, is called *The True Gospel of God of the Chinese*.

Even though this gospel had been written in ancient Chinese characters which are understood today only by Chinese language

---

1. See Chapter 8, first illustration.

schools, it was a book we knew we simply had to have. We asked Dr. Hsu if securing a copy would be possible. Dr. Hsu said it might be, provided the "powers" agreed, but, we were warned, to his knowledge no Caucasian had ever been conceded the honor.

Three nights later, he took us to the Society's headquarters (which, incidentally, are magnificent) in Taipei, where he had called a special meeting. The Chinese have a way of scrutinizing one which is little short of mental penetration and is most disconcerting.

The room we entered was a huge affair much like one of our own auditoriums, but without benefit of chairs; the oriental prefers to sit crosslegged on the floor. Near the room's center was a large oblong table on which were a number of brushes, some pots of vari-

Dr. Hsu, head of the Red Swastika Society, Taiwan.

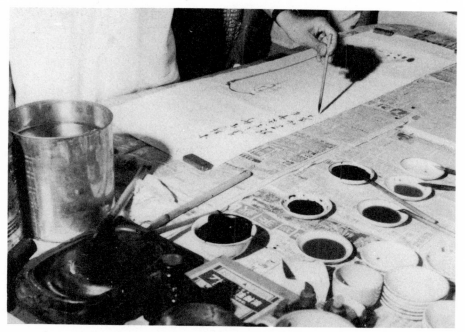

Automatic picture painting, the beginning of a "picture of prophesy."

ous colored paints, and long sheets of white paper. Toward the end of the room was an altar, and about the room numerous flickering lamps burned. Below one of these flaming lamps was displayed, within a glass case, the venerated book *The True Gospel of God of the Chinese.*

Our eyes darted from area to area. The faces that stared back at us seemed bleak and desolate. Dr. Hsu led us to the oblong table beside which now stood two men. One mixed paints furiously. With the addition of each new color, he bowed slightly in the direction of an urn in which smoldered sandalwood and five large sticks of incense. The scent permeated the room. The other man was apparently a medium of sorts; he gazed unblinkingly, trancelike, at the sheets of blank paper spread before him.

Dr. Hsu cautioned us to remain silent, and whispered that automatic symbolic picture painting was about to begin.

We felt every eye in that impressive room fixed in our direction, and our minds dwelt on the intriguing prospect of witnessing automatic picture painting. I had seen some examples of automatic writing performed in the States, but this was the first time I had ever

*The completion of a "picture of prophesy," Red Swastika
Society, Taiwan.*

heard of automatic picture painting. The Red Swastika Society practices this method as a means of prophesying, feeling that paintings
being formed in that way carry symbolic special meanings.

Suddenly the man with the trancelike stare grasped a brush and
began to paint, his hand moving with lightning swiftness. We mar-
veled at the beauty of the picture taking shape before our eyes. At
the speed it was being accomplished, it seemed utterly impossible.

There was a murmur from the others present. Our eyes shifted
to Dr. Hsu for a hint of the significance of the painting, but he also
stared as though hypnotized at the blurred hands of the artist as
they literally flew over the paper. The man was gazing, enraptured,
out into space yet there the picture was forming in perfect design
on the paper. His hands seemed controlled by a source outside of
himself. Then, sensing our bewilderment, the doctor softly stated
that the "High Spirits" were guiding the artist's hand.

Introduction

What seemed like an eternity, but which was actually no more than a few minutes, ended. The drawing was complete. We leaned forward.

"It is about you, "Dr. Hsu whispered. "You are mentioned in the painting!"

Others in the group carefully picked up the painting and brought it into an adjoining room, where it was hung. Another group of people gathered about and began to explain the symbolic painting. They did this in Chinese, but the courteous Dr. Hsu translated its meaning into English that we might understand. The symbolic contents of the entire painting are too lengthy for a detailed account here. Some of the contents referred to matters of importance to the Society and its members, but most important to us was the epoch-making announcement that the "powers" had agreed that we be permitted to have a copy of the sacred book and bring it back to the United States.

Fourteen days of intensive study and ceremonies later, *The True Gospel of God of the Chinese* was ours. Someday we hope to have it translated into English; it will be work for a scholar.

I will write further of The Red Swastika Society and show their "Picture of God" in a later chapter in this book.

For the beginning, come with me to the Philippine Islands and share with Ron and me our initial adventure on this journey into the unknown, as we enter the Quiapo.

Ron Ormond on the job.

IN THE PHILIPPINES

1

The "Black Nazareno" and the Miracles of Quiapo

The doctor's face took on a grave expression. He put his arm around the shoulder of Joseph Arcache, Sr., patted it gently, and proclaimed, "I'm sorry Joe, but your boy is dead."

The grief stricken father sank to the floor sobbing. "But why, but why . . . ?" was all he could utter.

"Spinal meningitis is a fatal disease," the doctor countered slowly. "As a doctor I did all I could. Nothing could have saved him but a miracle."

Joseph Arcache, Sr. rose from the floor slowly, painfully. His eyes fell on the still form of his five-year-old son lying there. In moments like this, Dr. Navarro found words hard to come by. All he could do was sympathize. Suddenly his eyes widened as the saddened father gathered up the motionless form of his young son, and, tenderly cradling him in his arms, walked slowly out of the room.

"Come back, come back," Dr. Navarro ordered. "You can do nothing now. No one can do anything."

But Dr. Navarro was wrong. He had not reckoned on a miracle, the miracle of Quiapo, where Arcache Senior took his son to lay his lifeless body at the foot of "The Black Nazareno" *and saw him live again!*

That was many years ago, and today Joseph Arcache, Jr. is a strong and healthy man living in Manila, one of thousands who are living proof that miracles can and do happen.

The "Miracle of Quiapo" is actually Quiapo itself. Located in the center of the teeming city of Manila, this gigantic church forms a fitting shrine for the housing of the world-famous Black Nazareno, or Black Jesus (pronounced Ha-soos), as it is affectionately called. The Black Jesus forms the devout center of worship, healing, and better being for hordes of people in the Philippines, who, in a steady stream, visit the shrine, which is credited with many thousands of miraculous cures during the history of its existence.

To learn the story of "The Black Nazareno," let us go back to the early forming of Quiapo itself. The Spanish Governor, General Santiago de Vera, founded the District of Quiapo on August 28, 1586, according to church records. Franciscan missionaries completed the first church of bamboo and nipa the same year. In 1636 it was burned to the ground, but rebuilding and repairs made to it at intervals created an edifice superior to the original.

Again in 1863 the Church of Quiapo was partially destroyed, this time by a disastrous earthquake. Two men of God, the Rev. Eusebio de Leon and Rev. Manuel Rexes, dedicated their services to its reconstruction, which was completed in 1899.

It was during the early part of the seventeenth century, according to the Church's history, that the black image of Christ was brought to Manila from Mexico by the Spaniards. The image was called "The Black Nazareno" then, just as it is today, for when it arrived it was already blackened, having been colored by the Mexican-Indian craftsmen who made the original carving in order to match the color of its native creators.

Because Quiapo was already under the charge of native Filipino clergy at the time of its arrival, the image was given to them, and from that time to the present it has been the object of ever-increasing pilgrimages, due undoubtedly to the constantly growing reputation of the miraculous cures experienced in its presence.

The first time Ron and I heard of Quiapo and "The Black Nazareno" was during a visit with Cosme Garcia, brother of the former President of the Republic of the Philippines.

"You have heard of our Black Nazareno at Quiapo?" he inquired. We confessed we had not.

"Then," said he, "I will take you there."

It was as simple as that. No pomp or ceremony. And it was in like manner that we met His Excellency Bishop Reyes, in whose parish Quiapo is located. Naturally, our first questions were of the miraculous cures that were reportedly occurring daily within the church.

"That is true," he replied simply.

"May we see a record of them," I asked next, thinking of the case histories of Lourdes that have been preserved.

"We have no records; keeping such would be impossible."

Thousands of people daily swarm before the Quiapo, responding to the call of their God.

Throngs flow into the Quiapo seeking the healing power of God through faith as they pray before the venerated "Black Nazareno."

His Eminence, Bishop Reyes of the Quiapo.

"Impossible?"

"If we recorded them in a book, soon the book would be filled, then we would acquire another book and another, and in time the entire church would be filled with—books," he said slowly. "What matters is not records but *healings*."

Ron and I listened intently, fascinated. Then:

"Have you ever witnessed a miracle?"

The question hit us like a bolt of lightning. We tried to mentally review the history of some of the strange and unusual manifestations we had studied. Both Ron and I remained silent, unsure.

"Come with me and I will show you," Bishop Reyes said quietly, as he turned to escort us into the church.

To try and convey a word-picture of Quiapo itself is superfluous.

Bishop Reyes and Ormond McGill.

It is built in the usual fashion of cathedrals, with, of course, certain embellishments typical in style to the Filipino. But to say that one can enter the shrine without the awe-inspiring feeling that he has entered a true house of God would be impossible.

"Rich man, poor man, beggar man, thief, women, children, people from every walk of life come to Quiapo; because Christ and Quiapo are impartial. All who wish may enter," the Bishop explained.

We noticed that there were three "Black Nazarenos" in Quiapo. One of Christ as He bore the cross, another of Christ as He hung upon the cross in crucifixion, and the third the image of Him in death, just prior to the ascension. We wondered which one of the three would be the most venerated. We asked the Bishop.

Answering our question, he replied, "Each one represents Christ, and no one is the more especially venerated."

We edged slowly over to the image of Christ in death. Of the three, we somehow found that one the most life-like and outstanding. As the three of us watched the throngs in prayer at His feet,

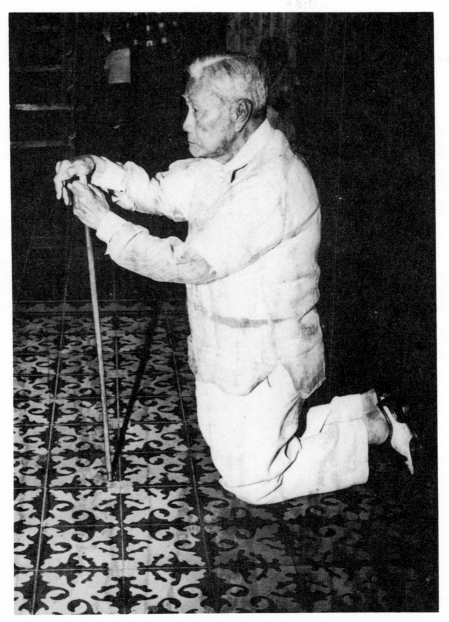

Joseph Arcache, Sr., on his weekly pilgrimage to the Quiapo, giving thanks for the miracle-cure of his son years before.

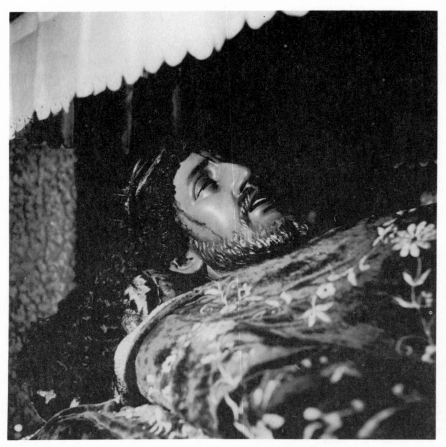

"The Black Nazareno."

feelings of reverence swarmed our minds and seemed to whisper, "He is not dead, He has risen and is the Savior of all mankind." It was almost as though we literally stood in the presence of the Master.

Later we were told that this particular "Nazareno" was the healer, and while the other two were credited also with miraculous cures, it was this image that attracted the hordes.

Our minds were busy with an array of details—questions about Quiapo and "The Black Nazareno,"—when Bishop Reyes broke our reverie. He directed our attention down the middle aisle of the church which was jammed with devotees, some crawling, others limping, many with children in their arms, making their way toward the image of Christ in death. Slowly, almost painfully, they

Worship at the feet of "The Black Nazareno," "The Healing Christ."

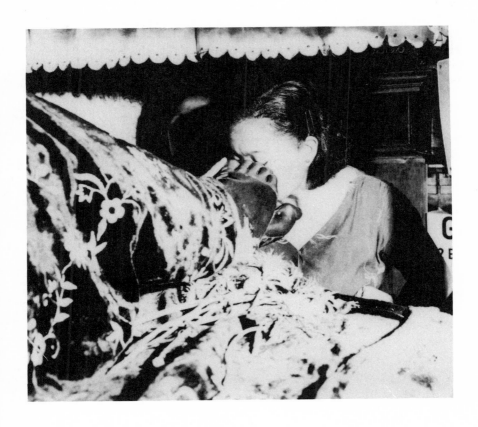

made their pilgrimage to the feet of Jesus' image. He pointed out one man in particular; a man well advanced in years.

That's Joseph Arcache, Sr.," the Bishop commented. "When his son was brought back to life by the Lord, he promised to come to Quiapo at least once each week. He has never broken that promise over many years."

It was then that we first heard the story of the miraculous resurrection of this man's son from death.

Our attention next went to another devotee half-dragging himself to the shrine. He had a crudely made crutch that helped him considerably as he hobbled along. Gently, reverently, he placed his hand upon the foot of the image while he sobbed convulsively. We, in turn, felt his emotion. Then he bravely tossed his home-made crutch into the corner among a heap of others, stood erect momentarily as though contemplating his next step, and, under his own power, walked out.

What is the power of "The Black Nazareno" that attracts the multitudes and obtains these cures? The answers vary according to the specific status of the knowledge of those who try to explain. The psychologist would say it is "the power of suggestion," the religious-minded might call it "the power of faith." His Excellency Bishop Reyes of the Quiapo quietly explains it as merely being a manifestation of the healing power of the living Christ, of which the image forms a focal point of veneration.

There is a tag to this story that commenced, oddly, even before Ron and I started the journey, and later led to our obtaining a replica of "The Black Jesus" for America. In the next chapter, I will tell of this incident, which was one of those rare happenstances that occasionally occur.

The Flagellantes

Once each year, at Easter, in remembrance of the suffering of Christ, this strange ritual is practiced in provincial areas of the Philippines. These devotees make promises of yearly penitence for their sins by marching through the streets flogging themselves with whips tipped with broken glass. Their faces are covered and their brows are wreathed in palm fronds symbolic of the "crown of thorns" worn by the Christ.

2

AOPSA and the Designing of the "Black Jesus" for America

When it was decided that we would make this trip to photograph strange religious mysteries of the Orient, it was obvious that if we were to successfully attempt to probe our cameras and investigations into the private business of unfamiliar people, we would have to have more to our purpose than merely making a motion picture. Religion is a very private business, more so in eastern countries than in western.

Thus, we formed with our wives, Delight McGill and June Ormond, and a group of understanding friends, a study association which we christened The American Oriental Paraphilosophical Study Associates. Shortened, called AOPSA.

We were all very sincere about this; the purpose of the group was to study and seek out truth in the fields of religious and esoteric learning, including the occult, psychic phenomena, comparative religions, metaphysics, and mystical teachings. Even more than study, we wanted to include in it something of a purpose aimed at perpetuating peace, harmony, and understanding between people of the Orient and those of the Occident. Accordingly, we drew up this basic code for the organization:

AOPSA believes that all great and true sages were in reality messengers from the same God, sent on earth at different times (or periods) to bring to all mankind His plan of salvation.

AOPSA believes in the philosophy of tolerance toward all religions that hold belief in the true God, by whatever name He may be called, Jehovah, Caodai, Tao, Allah, Brahma, or any other of the diversified names by which He may be identified to different peoples. In this manner, AOPSA aims to disseminate the principles of tolerance, liberty, equality, and fraternity to all mankind.

AOPSA believes in studying the teachings of the masters of all races and their variety of disciples, that through the combining of all such world-wide sources of learning may come a knowledge of the inner powers of man's divine heritage of mind and spirit that will bring him mastery of himself.

AOPSA believes in the careful disseminating of such insight to all people who have shown themselves of common mind, and who accept and believe in the five basic precepts of AOPSA:

A (aims) To praise the thought well thought, the word well spoken, and the deed well done.

O (omnipotence) To promote the wisdom of "oneness," and the sentiment of love toward one's neighbors.

P (propriety) To be kind to people and tolerant of things.

S (sincerity) To postulate universal peace as the highest ideal of mankind.

A (ambition) To let knowledge, wisdom, and understanding be our ever-present guides.

Forming AOPSA before we commenced our journey was one of the wisest things we ever did. It literally opened doors for us that otherwise would have forever remained closed. And not only did it promote our knowledge of the various subjects we sought to film, but it also proved a real bond of friendship with the many people we met along the way. In Manila, we had the official seal of the organization designed. In Hong Kong, the official pins were made. All were most interested in AOPSA. One might almost say that AOPSA actually formed a bond between people of East and West. It was amazing to us how this sincerity of purpose was responded to; we had many requests from oriental religious leaders to join the organization. They were fine people, and we were happy to have them do so.

It was AOPSA that led us to actually acquire a replica of "The Black Nazareno," exactly as it reposes in the famed Quiapo, and to bring the Black Jesus to America. I will tell of this happening.

As has been mentioned, there are three "Black Nazarenos" in the Quiapo. The original Black Jesus was imported from Mexico many years ago. There is a tale told of the remarkable peace surrounding the entire sea voyage during its transportation to the Philippines, as though the very elements remained bowed in respect. This figure shows Christ bearing the cross. It stands in the center of the church above the main altar and is taken, once each year at

The symbol of "AOPSA," as designed in the Philippines.

Easter, on parade through the streets of Manila in what has become known as "The Procession of the Black Nazareno." Thousands come to witness this event, and devotees fling themselves above the crowd to touch the hem of its garment as the figure passes by. Within the church a special staircase is arranged at the rear of the altar, that those seeking help may climb to the figure and touch its foot, which protrudes through a curtain draped behind the figure as it stands above the altar.

The second Black Jesus stands in a small room off to the right side of the front entrance of the church. This shows Christ on the cross in the conventional crucifix.

The third Black Jesus rests in a special canopy-covered casket near the left wall of the church as one faces the altar. This shows Christ in death after He had been taken off the cross prior to the resurrection. This is known as "The Healing Christ," to which the miracle of bringing life back to the dead and other miraculous cures are accredited.

All three figures are deeply venerated, but of the three, the one

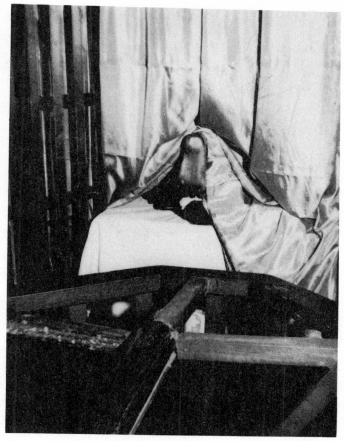

The foot of "The Black Nazareno," as it projects through the drapery behind the main altar at the front of the Quiapo. The wood of the carved foot is worn to a satin-smoothness from the caressing touches of thousands of devotees.

"The Christ in Death"—"The Black Nazareno," Quiapo, Philippine Islands.

that Ron and I felt most moved by was "The Healing Christ," so we requested permission of the officials of the church to have a replica of the figure created that this magnificent symbol of faith might be brought back to America.

It proved a monumental task, since the figure measures well over seven feet in length and presents Christ as a big man of strong physique. Even in death He is a most imposing figure of strength.

The figure is marvelously carved and shows our Lord as He rests in death after great suffering with all of the agonies and sorrows of mankind heaped upon His shoulders.

Bishop Reyes of the Quiapo gave his sanction that the new Black Jesus be made, and a special blessing was given the figure before its transporting to America.

Here in these pictures are shown the carving, construction, and shipping, through the auspices of AOPSA, of this remarkable religious artifact. The new Black Jesus is now in America, and it carries with it the same aura of compassion as does its counterpart still residing in the Philippine Islands. There is a "power" about the figure, for the power of "The Healing Christ" is the power of faith —in our Lord, Jesus the Christ.

I will tell next of another adventure in the Philippines which deals with healing in the name of Christianity, but in an even stranger way. Come with us to San Fabian, which is in the back country one hundred and fifty miles north of Manila.

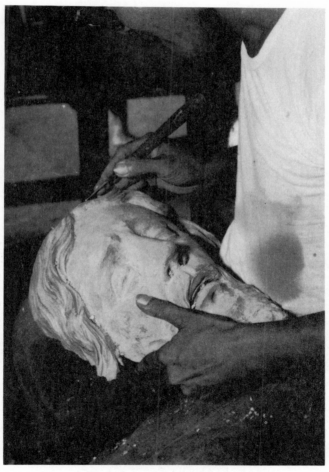

The carving of the new *"Black Nazareno."*

*Craftsmen of the Clemente de Jesus E. Hijo family, skilled arti-
sans of religious carving, on sanction of the Quiapo, reproduce
in exact detail the figure of "The Black Nazareno."*

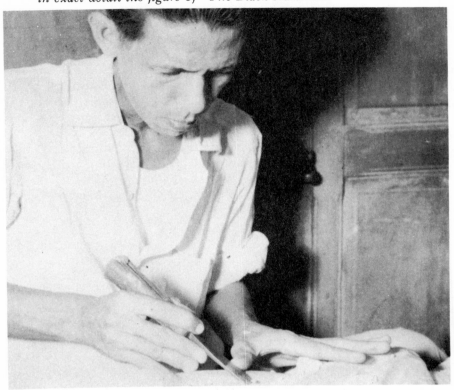

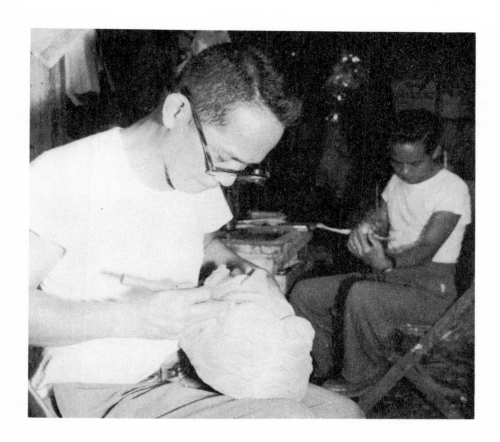

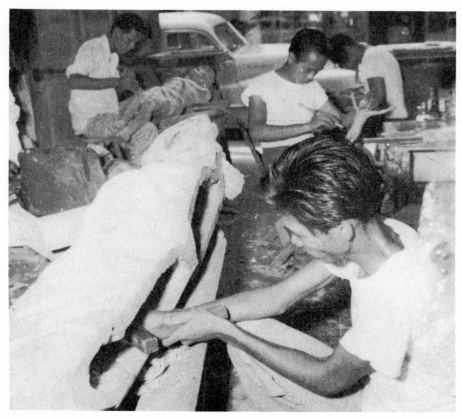

Ormond McGill and Ron Ormond inspect the carving of "The Black Nazareno."

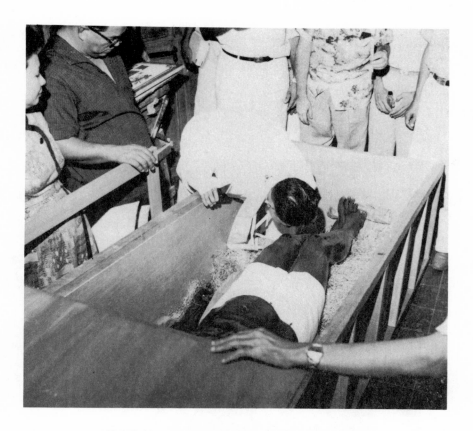

Official blessing of the new "Black Nazareno."

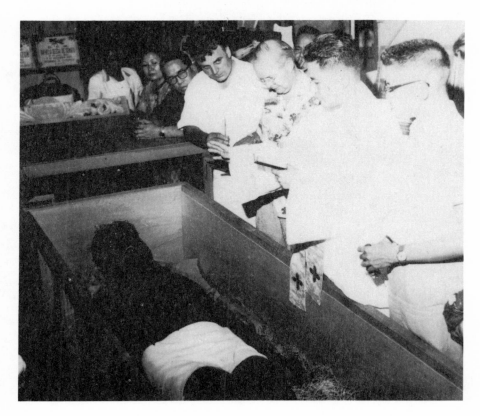

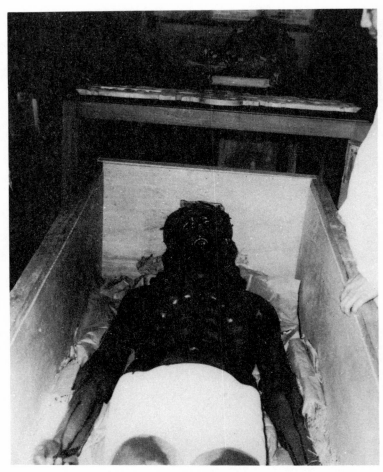

The remarkable replica of "The Black Nazareno," crated and ready for shipment to the United States.

3

Terte, the Fourth Dimensional Surgeon, and his Amazing Operations

It was while visiting the home of Guillesmo Tolentino in Manila that Ron and I reached a decision to photograph Terte, the fourth-dimensional surgeon. Of course, our host did not refer to him by any such science fiction nom de plume. That was my own invention. But what he appeared to do definitely belongs in that category.

Guillesmo Tolentino is a highly respected man, and is one of the most renowned sculptors in the Philippines, possibly in the world. He is also a leader and devoted member of The Union Espiritist Cristiana de Filipinas, the Christian Spiritualistic Society of the Philippine Islands. When he showed us an amateur motion picture he had made of the wonderman's operations he galvanized us to action; we could hardly wait to get our own camera's lens in front of Terte's amazing hands. For the hands of Terte are wonderful things, and truly have remarkable healing powers. However he does it, we know for a fact that cures occur in great numbers in his remote healing center way up in San Fabian. I will have Ron tell of this adventure.

The lens of my movie camera was barely inches away from the heaving abdomen of the pain-ridden woman, as the little Filipino's fingers seemed to disappear into her flesh with no more effort than a brush being dipped into a bucket of paint.

47

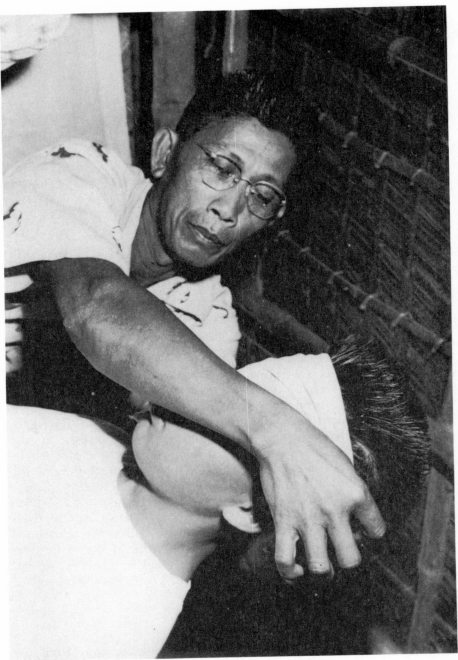

Terte, "The Fourth-Dimensional Surgeon."

I stared through the viewfinder, not daring to believe what I saw, as the fingers slowly withdrew clutching what seemed to be a greenish, poison-loaded appendix. The woman whose diseased organ had just been so magically removed sighed with relief, and, at a signal, slowly rose to a sitting position.

When I released the camera trigger and straightened, the woman was smiling at Eleuterio Terte, who is listed in Filipino governmental records as a farmer living at San Fabian, Pangasinan. Other sources, including government medical officials, unofficially list him as a charlatan. But they haven't been able to prove this contention.

I stared openly at this quiet, unassuming Filipino, standing shirtless, perspiring, waiting for his next patient to stretch out on the makeshift operating table. The woman whose appendix apparently had been removed in this bloodless, mysterious operation already had joined her friends and relatives, who were questioning her in low, awe-filled tones. She seemed perfectly at ease, showing no sign of the pain which had engulfed her only moments before.

I was perspiring almost as heavily as Terte, and my hands were shaking. Ormond McGill, my partner, stepped up and I turned to look at him, showing my puzzlement.

The assurance I hoped to see in his eyes, however, was absent. He was fully as mystified by what had just happened as I.

"What about it?" I wanted to know.

He shook his head.

We had heard of Eleuterio Terte while in Manila, and at first were inclined to doubt the authenticity of the wonders credited to his, as Mac dubbed them, fourth-dimensional powers to heal. Mac, however, took it upon himself to check with local newspapers and compile clippings on the San Fabian faith healer. He had discovered that Terte's followers were not simple rabble, but included an impressive array of lawyers, college students, professional people and businessmen.

Terte, we learned, had come to Quezon City to offer his healing powers to the ill and diseased. He promptly had become the target of scoffing medical school graduates.

Carrying out his healing processes at nightly meetings, he soon found himself termed a hoax by Dr. Petronio Monsod, health officer of Quezon City. The good doctor even urged Philippine's Health Director, Felipe Arenas, to have the farmer-turned-healer jailed.

With the backing of the Union Espiritists Cristiana de Filipinas, Terte countered the approaching threat by offering to conduct one of his unique curative sessions before a panel of recognized physicians, public officials, and, if desired, minions of the law. He would remove an inflamed appendix, or perform a similar feat in major surgery through the simple expedient of passing a finger into the patient's body and bringing forth the infected organ.

Terte and his followers didn't even receive the courtesy of a formal reply to this offer. Instead, he was raided by the police. But upon the arrival of the officers, Terte had disappeared. He had returned to his farm in San Fabian, apparently disgusted and unhappy with the results of his pilgrimage to Quezon City.

Some of this Mac and I had learned in Manila, the rest in Quezon City. We discussed at length whether it would be worth our time and the expense involved to investigate further. It was Guillermo Tolentino, the great artist, who was responsible for our decision.

Tolentino told us that Terte is president of the San Fabian chapter of the Union Espiritista Cristiana de Filipinas, a Christian group of occultists boasting 148 centers scattered throughout the Island Republic with more than one million members.

The organization is largely a spiritualist group, but unlike many others in the Far East, its doctrine has its basis in the Christian religion. The term utilized by the group, in translation, means "spiritist," and departs from spiritualism as we know it in certain facets. The spiritist mediums are more than "middle men," who pass on messages from the celestial world, according to Tolentino. Many, like Terte, are possessed of the gift of healing.

Such claims, of course, are not new. The great shrines at Lourdes in France and St. Anne de Beaupre in Canada have their fame built upon their curative powers for those who make the pilgrimage. There have been myriad faith healers through the ages, most of whom drew their powers from good, others from evil, if the records are to be believed.

Terte, according to Tolentino, had first discovered his power of healing in 1950 as the result of *spiritual illumination,* and had been removing tonsils, kidneys and gall stones, as well as fatty material surrounding an enlarged heart, curing the afflicted for a year prior to his ill-fated mission to Quezon City.

After his self-banishment to his farm following that incident, he had deliberately shunned publicity, covering a circuit near his home some 250 kilometers north of Manila. However, he was seemingly agreeable to treating any who were willing to come to his farm, where, on weekends, he held sessions in a sizeable thatch-walled room.

Tolentino also showed McGill and myself a thesis written by Senorita Teresa C. Goba while studying for her master-of-arts degree. It deals with drugless healing and lists certain of Terte's accomplishments which she documented. Included in these cases were the removal of an appendix from Segundo Talag, son of a physician, the removal of kidney stones from Professor Toma Aguirre, the purging of the fatty tissue from the chest cavity of one Acela Franco, who suffered an enlarged heart, and the treatment of a stomach tumor from the body of Jose Libunao. Senorita Goba had interviewed each of these former patients and was able to state that they considered themselves cured.

We wanted to check the matter ourselves.

Contact was made with the healer through Tolentino, who told us that Terte agreed to let us film the entire day's proceedings.

We hired a driver to take us to San Fabian and made the 250 kilometers from Manila overnight. The car was a 1949 Ford, which bore the bullet holes of rebel actions and other marks of the violence which seems to lie smoldering throughout the Islands. In spite of its outward appearance, however, the vehicle seemed to have an excellent engine and was otherwise in good repair. We were forced to pack our cameras and sound equipment in the back seat with us. The trunk carried several G.I. water cans filled with gasoline. The odor of the fuel semed to seep through from the trunk to the interior of the car, and both Mac and I glanced dubiously at our Filipino driver, as he ignored the smell of gas fumes and lit up a thick cigar.

Driving through the night, Mac and I tried to sleep, but it was little use. Sections of the road were torn up and the rest was just bumpy. Every time I'd doze off, I would be brought wide awake by the sensation of the Ford driving down a well!

"What a trip," McGill remarked, not too happily, after he had been jostled awake by a particularly jolting fall into a set of ruts.

It was morning when we arrived in San Fabian. Our driver asked directions to Terte's farm. We had to get a *caratella* (small horse-drawn wagon) to go the rest of the way. On this point our car driver objected, but, after making the transfer, we were all soon bumping along a country lane.

Our driver gave us a strange glance, and I couldn't help wondering whether he was trying to diagnose our particular ailments.

San Fabian was a typical rural Philippine community with entire families cultivating the few acres that make them a meager living. Terte's farm was no different than the others, his home a palm frond-covered shack raised off the ground. In the rear, however, was a long low building which served as a meeting hall. While most of those present were farmers and laborers from the surrounding district, there also was a sprinkling of business and professional men from as far away as Manila.

The meeting opened with singing and readings from the Bible in the Tagalog dialect, a part of which was explained by our driver who was serving as our interpreter. These sermons were delivered for the most part by assistants of Terte.

Terte, a rather small, slender man with a gentle, quiet face then rose to deliver his own sermon.

Our driver-interpreter explained that the sermons covered the basic theme of the Fraternity of Spiritists; the believers are referred to as a brotherhood rather than a religion, as members belong to virtually every religious denomination to be found in the Far East. The basic creed is God, His law and His love. Its aim is world peace based upon the Fatherhood of God and the brotherhood of all men.

I had been watching the proceedings quietly, noting an atmosphere of peace and faith which had come over the group. Mac, beside me, had settled down, although I knew that he was wound up like a spring waiting for the healing demonstrations to start.

The unkind articles I had read in the press files, written in 1951, had made jibing reference to the trances into which Terte put himself before performing an operation. Apparently the reporter had gone overboard in his description, because the healer used no such preparation. Approximately three hundred persons were present at the services that Sunday morning, and at least two-thirds had come to be cured.

One of Terte's first ceremonial acts was to bless the water which had been brought to the operating tables in bowls, jars, bottles, and pans by members of the gathering. Both Mac and I tasted the water as it was placed there. There was nothing unusual about it. It was just water.

In sanctifying the water, Terte read scriptural passages from the Tagalog Bible, extending his hands over the containers with fingers pointing downward. As I watched closely, his face remained calm, almost stoic, but his lower arms seemed to swell, muscles and veins protruding, knotting, as though some unseen force were creeping down into his fingers seeking release.

Suddenly the water began to take on a pinkish color and there was a stir of excitement from the onlookers. McGill was watching closely, face twisted in concentration that was almost as deep as that on the features of the healer.

"Could be a chemical reaction," he whispered.

"But did you see him drop in anything?"

Mac didn't answer. I knew he had not. And, with his experience as a magician, I was certain he would have seen any chemical powder or any other substance that might have drifted down from Terte's fingers to cause the pink clouding effect.

"What's that for?" I asked our driver. It was explained that the water, once sanctified, could be taken home and drunk to protect one from diseases or even evil spirits.

The idea of a Christian people believing in evil spirits may seem

The "sanctifying of the water" by Terte, a ceremony preceding every healing session of the startling operations. Dozens of vessels, containing water brought by devotees, are treated, as Terte directs the healing force out of his fingertips.

Ron Ormond takes a sip of the "sanctified water."

strange to many people in the West, but in the Philippines, the orientals have been able to intertwine the age-old beliefs with the newer aspects of religion which they have come to accept.

Those seeking treatment had earlier been registered by Terte's volunteer assistants, and now awaited their turns. Before the first, a man suffering from what they called a "cataract," could be summoned, I glanced at McGill who was looking about the dim confines of the thatch hall. At my urging, the interpreter asked the healer if his operating table could be moved out into the sunlight so we could make better use of the color film with which our movie footage was to be shot.

A look of satisfaction came over Mac's face. He was no more surprised than I, however, when Terte readily agreed to such a move. In the open sunlight, any props or trick gadgets he might have had within the hall would not be present. Also, if his operations were dependent upon sleight-of-hand, it would be much more detectable.

Terte stood by quietly as some of his followers moved the operating table through the narrow door and set it up in the sun. It was little more than a long wooden rack covered by a thin pad.

As the man with the "cataract" took his place on the table, Terte stepped forward, rubbing alcohol over his hands and flexing his fingers carefully. A hush settled over those looking on. As before, I noted the knotting of muscles in his forearm and the manner in which the veins stood out.

A special interpreter, who had been assigned to us as a follower of the healer, explained that Terte "operates" only when he feels the spiritual power of God enter him, feeling it throughout his entire body, particularly in his fingers, which become almost hot and exceedingly supple.

A small choir of five girls had come to stand behind the healer, and, when he commenced to work, began singing a melodic but repetitious chorus. We were informed this was called "The Healing Song." Quite an interesting song; as I photographed, Mac took it down on our tape recorder.

Terte first placed a cloth, dampened with the sanctified water, across the patient's eyes. I was at work steadily with the camera, the lens tipped down upon the face of the patient, listening to the whirr of film running through the sprockets, as I watched the action through the viewfinder. Mac, holding the mike of the tape recorder, was at my shoulder, his breath coming in uneven gulps.

Slowly the cloth was raised and Terte seemed to poke his forefinger and thumb directly into the man's eye. Watching the patient, I expected him to flinch or show some sign of pain. Not a muscle in his face quivered.

I muttered under my breath in amazement, as Terte seemed to

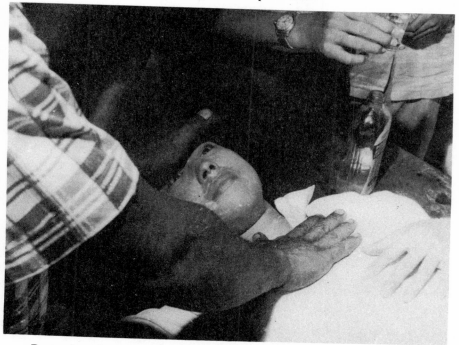

Preparing the patient before the operation. The soothing hands of Terte are placed on the patient's forehead, removing all pain.

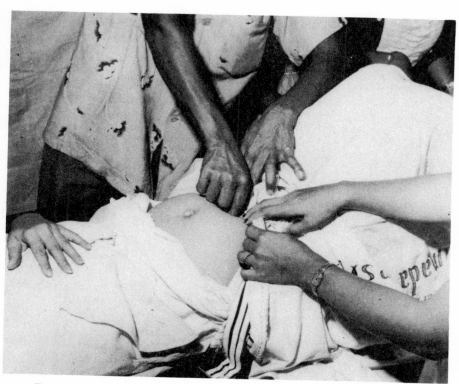

Terte's wonderful hands as they begin to reach within the body to remove a diseased part.

The extracted diseased tissue is placed in a jar of alcohol and carefully preserved.

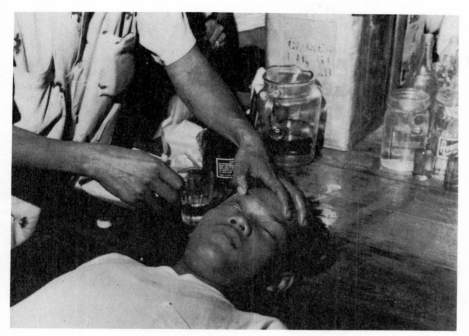

Terte performing a cataract operation

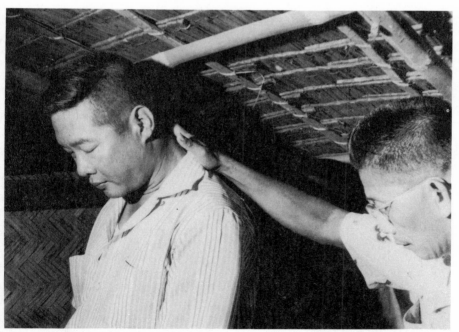

Terte applying the curing powers of "the laying-on-of-hands" to the abcess on the neck of Francisco Cisep.

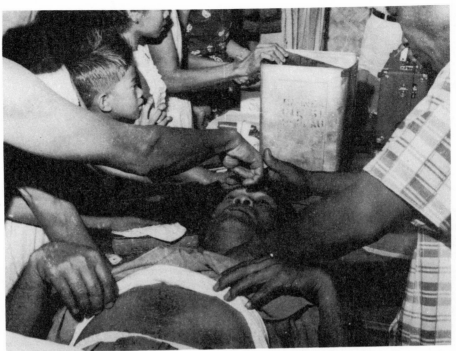

The patient, ready to arise from the table after a spiritual operation. No pain is experienced and the patient walks away apparently healed.

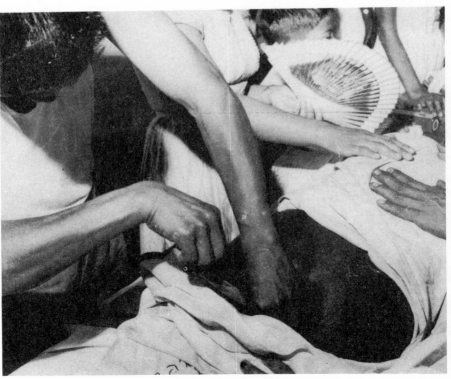

Terte removing a foreign object from the rectum of a patient believed to be bewitched.

lift the "cataract" from the afflicted eye, dropping it into a jar of alcohol extended toward him by an aide. He handed the jar to the patient, who walked away apparently cured.

The next patient was Francisco Cisep, a well-known Chinese businessman of Manila, who was suffering from a huge, angry-looking, boil-like sore on the back of his neck. The running sore had refused to heal.

There was no sign of pain from the man as Terte touched the infection. Terte went through much the same ritual as before. When Cisep rose from the treatment, I looked closely at the back of his neck. The badly inflamed section had almost disappeared. All that remained were a few dry flakes clinging to the skin.

"Unbelievable!" Mac breathed in my ear. He was echoing my own sentiments.

At first, Terte wore a light cotton shirt and I knew that McGill was watching those sleeves, turned back at the wrists, but there was no sign of the magician's art. In time, the little man had perspired so much that the shirt was hanging on him in dripping folds. He quietly removed it and went on with his work, arms bare, body, trunk and chest covered only by a thin undershirt.

A patient suffering from what had been diagnosed as a gallstone lay on the table, abdomen bared. Terte's thumb and forefinger of his right hand sunk out of sight into the flesh. As his fingers disappeared within the man, the choir commenced their singing, stopping only when the healer's hands emerged with the gallstone, which was dropped into the waiting jar of alcohol.

In each operation, there appeared to be no pain, no bleeding, no open wound of any kind. In one instance, during a spiritual operation, both Mac and I thought we saw a smear of blood on the patient. Moments later, though, any such signs had disappeared.

Another patient had removed what was allegedly a bit of diseased liver. Whatever it was, when he arose, the ill man showed the high flush of health replacing what had previously been a sickly pallor.

Throughout the afternoon, as the sun beat down unmercifully, many more persons joined the crowd of three hundred that had attended the morning service. Several hundred patients passed, one by one, before "the fourth-dimensional surgeon" of San Fabian that long day. Some he rejected with a shake of his head as they came forward; others he beckoned to lie on the table for immediate operation. The healer's body was coated with a film of sweat, but the aloof serenity of his face never changed. And among his operations he occasionally treated some bewitchment cases as well.

Later, one of Terte's assistants and followers, a young man named Juan Enbarnal, took over to extract some teeth. The first

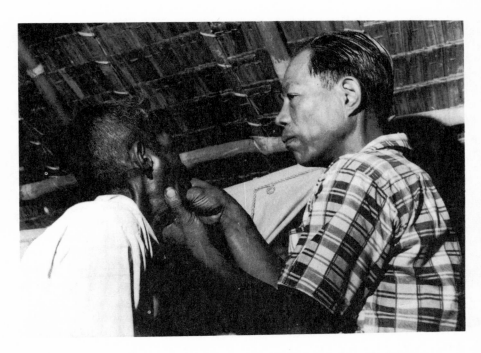

Terte's assistant, Juan Enbarnal, extracting teeth with his bare fingers during the strange healing session at San Fabian, Philippines.

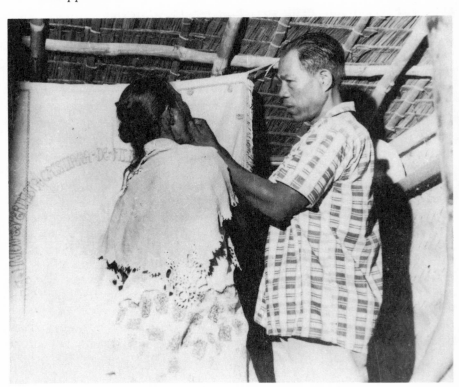

person upon whom he "operated" was in obvious pain from a visibly abcessed molar. Yet the patient seemed to feel no pain as Enbarnal's fingers touched the tooth.

Mac was at the healer's elbow, watching every move, while I shot over his shoulder with the camera. There was an audible clicking sound as the tooth was released from the jawbone, yet the young man's thumb and forefinger seemed to touch it with the most gentle of caresses. Both of us examined the tooth, new and raw, then examined the gaping hole where the tooth had been. There was a drop of blood on the gum. The patient drank some of the sanctified water, then joined the crowd, his pain now gone.

Later, speaking through our interpreter, we were allowed to interview patients picked at random. All appeared healthy, and were convinced Terte had performed a miracle. *Or rather, that* God *had performed the miracle, using Terte as* His *instrument.* Such is the way that Terte himself, as well as his followers, explained the "operations."

Ron Ormond recording at the healing session.

An interview with the amazing "Fourth-Dimensional Surgeon,"
following the spiritual operations.

"I can do nothing unless the power of the Spirit Protector is
within me," the fourth-dimensional surgeon stated.

We asked other questions, too, looking for the gimmick. How
much did they intend to give Terte for the healings? Give, perhaps,
to the church of their individual faith, give to God, but certainly
not to Terte. He not only didn't want it, it was not his to accept
even if he did.

With five sons working his farm, Terte, they say, has no need
for their money, and were he to accept any for the miracles, the
power would soon leave him.

We were amazed. The possibility that Terte had planted people
for our benefit didn't hold water. It would hardly be logical for
him to have a hundred confederates, and what of the other thousands who claimed he had cured them of illnesses—the lawyers, pro-
fessors, and reputable businessmen?

That evening, as we drove back toward Manila, McGill was

strangely quiet, staring down at the stacks of exposed movie film in cans at our feet.

"What's your verdict?" I asked.

He hesitated for a long moment, then shook his head, not looking up.

"One of two things. Either that man's working miracles or he's the greatest magician that ever lived."

As Ron Ormond mentions, witchcraft is very much believed in and accepted in the Philippines, and Terte comes in for his share of the curing of bewitchments which are looked upon by the people of these islands as a disease like any other.

Those who have read my book, *The Secret World of Witchcraft,* will recall mention made of "projective magic," in which a foreign object is projected by the witch into the body of the victim, producing very harmful effects and frequently death. It is the business of the witch doctor to cure the patient by magically removing the object.

During the course of the day, I saw Terte perform such operations, interspersed among the more conventional ones, in which gross material such as large splinters of wood, balls of dried grass and such were removed from the body of the ill person lying before him.

It is difficult for occidentals to appreciate how seriously these people accept disease by witchcraft, and were Terte to reject such practice he would not fully be doing his job for his particular clientele. Terte is a strange man, part Christian healer and part witch doctor.

There is not the slightest doubt that remarkable spiritual healings occur at San Fabian. Faith and belief are powerful there, and there is the strong psychological impact of the amazing extractions. Also, Terte and his followers place much emphasis on the ancient manner of curing the sick by the "laying-on-of-hands." In the next chapter, I will present some of my personal observations on this interesting technique of which Terte was a master.

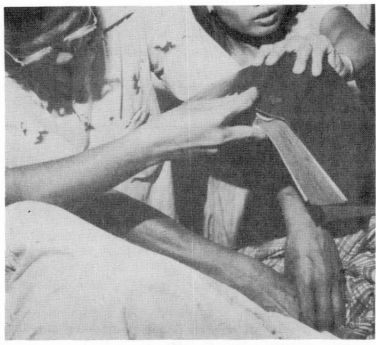

Closeup of the miraculous hands of Terte, "The Fourth-Dimensional Surgeon." The Word of God (the Tagalog Bible) is present at every operation, held canopy-like over the patient, while a choir of girls chants "The Healing Song."

4

"Laying-on-of-Hands" and Spiritual Healing

Spiritual healing of the sick, of which the "laying-on-of-hands" is a major method, has been closely associated with religion throughout history. Paramount among such healings are those reported to have been performed by Christ. And many other persons of spiritual faith down through the centuries have performed cures in His name. That such "miracles" occur is proven fact, but the causation of the cures has been the subject of much speculation.

Depending upon the point-of-view of the investigator, such healings usually fall into these categories:

1. PSYCHOLOGICAL: the ailments being regarded as psychosomatic and being aided by the psychotherapeutic use of techniques such as suggestion and hypnosis.
2. MAGNETIC HEALING: treatments in which the operator (or healer) appears to give a quantity of his own "vital force" to the patient, resulting in well-being and the removal of the disease.
3. FAITH HEALING: in which remarkable healing occurs as the result of the strong belief (faith) of the patient. Such cures are observed frequently at sacred shrines such as Lourdes in France and the Quiapo in the Philippines.
4. MIRACLES FROM GOD: healing as a direct manifestation of God.

As a professional hypnotist, I have been especially interested in

The wonderful hands of Terte, which, he states, manifest the healing power of God.

the subject of spiritual healing and have spent considerable time in its research. As a result of my study, I am inclined to feel that all four of these aspects occur simultaneously (in varying degrees, of course) in such "miraculous cures." In this chapter, I will consider the subject with a brief historical outline, and then go into the most interesting aspect of these healing manifestations, the practice of the "laying on of hands" technique.

What is known as hypnotism, under a variety of names, is a very ancient art and has been practiced, in one form or another, in every country of the world by witch doctors, medicine men, shamans, priests and mystics.

In ancient Greece, at the Temple of Aesculapius, god of medicine, the sick were put into trances by priests, saw visions of the gods, and were cured. Grecian oracles and prophetesses foretold events while in self-induced hypnotic states.

In India, the fakir renders himself oblivious to pain and plunges daggers through his flesh, or sleeps on a bed of nails. Yogis have been buried alive and later revived without bodily harm. In the South Seas, natives, in trance-like ecstasy, dance on red-hot coals in the famous "fire walks." The Persian Magi, the Mongols, Tibetans, and the Chinese all had knowledge of the power called hypnotism.

In the late 18th century, Dr. Franz Anton Mesmer, a Viennese physician, observed certain "faith cures" and became very interested in the phenomena. He reasoned that such cures must be caused by the passing of some unknown force between the healer and the patient. He conjectured that the human body had two poles, like a magnet, and that an invisible magnetic fluid is given off by the body. Thus the term *animal magnetism* was created.

Despite many successful cures by his processes, Mesmer's work was not well received in Vienna. After being warned by the authorities to discard his unorthodox methods, he left Vienna and moved to Paris in 1778, where he quickly created a vogue for mesmeric treatment among the French aristocracy.

Mesmer began to make a fortune, much to the envy of fellow physicians who eventually persuaded the French government to order an official investigation of his practices. The report most undeservedly branded Mesmer a fraud, despite his successful results with hundreds of patients. He left France and eventually returned to his native Austria, where he died in 1815.

James Braid, a surgeon of Manchester, England, was attracted to Mesmer's work and pursued his own experiments. He found that he could induce a trance-like state through a fixation of the eyes and the use of suggestion, without need for any special "magnetic fluid." He coined the name "hypnotism" for this state, taking it from the Greek word *hypnos*, meaning sleep. Yet Braid definitely stated that the phenomena produced by his process and that produced by Mesmer were not one and the same, and that much of the strange psychic experiences and cures reported through the use of animal magnetism could not be obtained by hypnosis.

My own studies rather substantiate Braid's views, and, as I have observed in the operation of the "laying on of hands" process in many countries, there does, indeed, seem to be a transference of some "vital energy" from the operator to the patient that is important to the curing of the disease. Be it known as spiritual healing or (as it was named by Mesmer), "magnetic healing," (synonymous with animal magnetism), it seems to be a generalized healing force, a God-given spiritual gift generated by the nervous system of the human body, directed by the mind, and created by the spirit. I will elaborate upon my findings.

Persons who practice the "laying-on-of-hands" state that they can actually feel the passage of a vital force from their body into the patient. Some refer to this as a magnetic power, but most I have spoken to in the Orient refer to the practice of "The God Power in The Hands." Despite the difference in names, all seem to have a surprisingly similar viewpoint about what it is, how it operates, and how to use it, including a basic belief that every human being has a power which can be developed by practice to the point of curing disease in himself and in others by the application of this vital force. This power is considered a life-energy transferred by the healer to the patient as his hands are laid upon the individual. The energy works directly upon the nervous system of the patient, and its healthful influence is then communicated to the brain. It is a spiritual force, which is probably why it has been closely associated with various forms of religion by those "in rapport" with God, so to speak.

I have asked such healers if they did not feel that their practices might interfere with the work of more scientific methods of therapy used by the medical profession. All have answered most sincerely that they in no way discourage the use of orthodox medical methods, but wish their treatment to be regarded entirely as an adjunct of a psychic and spiritual nature, as a technique which complements modern medical practice in man's constant struggle to combat and overcome disease.

There are certain beliefs that every magnetic healer holds. Every human is regarded as magnetic, constantly attracting and repelling. This attraction and repulsion is unconscious. The practice of magnetic healing is strictly the practice of using this continuous magnetic force *consciously*, that is to say, projecting it upon others by determined effort of will. The hands are looked upon as the instruments through which the energy is transmitted; the right hand being the positive hand and the left hand the negative. In the practice of the "laying-on-of-hands," the intent is to transmit the vital energy (or "magnetism," as some call it) to the patient by means of the application of the right hand, using the left hand to "close the circuit"; that is, to very strongly draw the current through the patient's body from the right hand to the left.

As to where this force is created, healers look upon the human body as a laboratory for the manufacture of this magnetic force; it is ever there to be drawn upon and directed as is desired; it is energy from the inner reservoir of man. Spiritual healers have a beautiful philosophy that the more freely one gives, the more freely one receives, and whereas the average man, who is only unconsciously magnetic, gives off very little personal magnetism in his daily intercourse with other human beings and reabsorbs very little magnetism into his own nervous system, the magnetic healer makes a daily practice of assisting his fellows and in return receives a special influx of vital energy from the quickened assimilation of the practice. In other words, when one is determined to help others, he so quickens the vibration of his own organism that he receives supplies of strength from the inexhaustible source in proportion to the demand. No selfish person can be a really successful magnetic healer. Mastery comes with sincerity of purpose and love of one's fellow man.[1]

Oriental spiritual healers express it this way: the "power" is unending, since it springs from the God-source within. The more it is called upon the greater the flow.

The mental concentration of the healer seems to have importance in the "laying on of hands." Healers in eastern countries seem to prefer to develop a serene state of mind and concentrate on the inner flow of force passing down their arms, out their fingertips, and on into the patient. Healers in western countries seem more inclined to hold in their minds thoughts related to the direct curing of the specific disease to which attention is being directed. I have tried both procedures, and personally prefer the oriental, as I feel that it is the flow of vital force that is important to pass into the patient, who, in turn, will automatically use it where it is most needed to help his body. With practice comes sensitivity, and in the passing of the "magnetism" one can feel a sort of flow down the arms and a tingling in the fingertips as it flows out.

The placement of the hands on the patient varies with different spiritual healers. Some simply grasp the hands of the patient in theirs and pass the vital flow along from hands across to hands. Others stand before the patient and grip the head at the temples in a squeeze between the hands. Still others prefer to place their hands directly over the diseased part of the body, that the "force" may enter that area directly. The old mesmeric technique was to pass the "force" along to the patient without direct contact at all, using long, sweeping passes over the entire length of the body while keeping the hands at a distance of about six inches from its surface. Upward passes were used to first remove the diseased "magnetism" from the person, this being then discarded by rapid flicking of the hands in the air to disperse it. Downward passes were then used to renew the patient with fresh "vital fluid."

As to what method of projection-contact is best, here again I am of the opinion that it makes little difference. All methods cause the vital force to pass from the body of the healer into the body of the patient to be used as needed. To me, the rationale of healing via "laying-on-of-hands" is that an ill person is low in his vital force,

---

1. That the "laying-on-of-hands" principle applies a vital energy rather than the purely psychological seems evident from the fact that animals may be healed by the same process as humans. Some persons seem to have a special talent (or gift) for such healing. Generally speaking, however, I am inclined to believe that the more the "power" is used, the more it develops.

and the healer provides him with an additional supply that is used to effect the healing.

Despite the fact that "laying-on-of-hands," as a method of curing the sick, has been used for centuries and countless cures testify to its effectiveness, until recently western science was extremely skeptical. Today, some investigators are not so sure, now that the human aura and various unsuspected body radiations are beginning to be registered. I rather suspect that "laying on of hands" will follow a pattern similar to that of acupuncture as practiced by the Chinese. Here was an age-old art of healing looked upon as superstition until some medical experimenters had the courage to test it. Much to the surprise of the western world, fact was found behind what was thought to be fiction. And with investigation the "laying on of hands" may also prove to have a basis in scientific fact.

In the Philippine Islands there are sparsely-explored areas inhabited by aborigines. Some of them are headhunters. Their religious belief, in common with most primitive peoples, is animism, and they are said to have some unusual psychic powers and practice divination. I will tell of our adventures among the aborigines of the Philippines in the next chapter.

5

Animism and Psychical Phenomena in the Philippines

As animists, the aborigines hold the belief that all objects possess a natural life or vitality, or are endowed with indwelling souls—souls that animate all things. In this they are expressing, in a rudimentary way, the philosophical thought that there is *something* that is the essence of all creation, and, as such, is present in all things; objects both animate and inanimate.

For instance, the Mois of North Vietnam, the Ifugaos of the Philippines, and the Was and Shans of Burma, along with the other aboriginal peoples of the world, believe that a log or sizable chunk of wood has a soul, and that it becomes a much more powerful entity when it is carved into a figure or mask, since its indwelling spirit is given special opportunity to manifest itself. This is the basic magic of icons and masks. Such artifacts, believers say, bring spiritual power, put there by the Great Spirit, to the owner.

A witch doctor or medicine man is an integral part of every tribe, regardless of its size. However, since the term "witch" might be misconstrued, the term "medicine man" is preferred. Although witches, as such, are frowned upon by aborigines, they admit to their existence.

There are so many different tribes of aborigines scattered over the Philippines, Southeast Asia, the Pacific Islands, and other remote areas of the world, each with their own particular variety of animistic worship, that a detailed reporting of such rituals would entail a work in itself. For the present purpose, it will be sufficient to give the reader a personal observation of religio-magic as practiced by the Ifugao tribe in the Philippines.

71

If one delves back into the history of the Etruscans, mention is made of the practice of reading the future by heiromancy, i.e., of a seer inspecting the entrails of sacrificed beasts by handling their warm liver and spleen. In the Bontoc area where the Ifugaos live, the performance of heiromany is regarded as sacred and is called a *cañao*. It is related to their religion. They have a variety of *cañaos*, depending upon the purpose aimed at by the medicine man. The one I will describe here, and that Ron was able to photograph, is a diagnostic cañao.

First a sacrifice is prepared by the offering of a couple of chickens and a pig. The chickens are killed and their blood made to drip into a bowl of half a coconut shell. Then the pig is killed by a process that spills not a single drop of blood; a small slit is made in the fatty tissue, and through this slit a needle-sharp bamboo sliver is plunged directly into the heart, causing instant death. Next the viscera is removed from both the chickens and the pig, and the shape of the liver and position of the gall bladder is carefully examined for good omens. The medicine man, in his inspection of these or-

Preparing a sacrifice for Ifugao divination ceremonial cañao.

gans, conducts his perusal in much the same manner that a palmist does in going over the lines in the hands of a client.

Thus, the condition and position of the organs is used for divination; a normal gall bladder being a good omen, a sign that the prayers given have been heard. The normal is good, the abnormal is bad; quite a logical philosophy. The medicine man thus completes his diagnosis of the illness of the sick one, and the ceremony is finished. Treatment is then administered according to the "reading."

Ron took both motion pictures and stills of the whole thing; following the ceremony the fun really began as the entire village partook of a feast. The gay mood seemed conducive to dancing, but none was allowed as that would have required the sacrificing of three pigs, while but one was used in this instance. Dancing is held as a sort of rite with religious significance to the aborigines.

These natives are known as headhunters, and many to whom I have told our adventures asked if the visit was dangerous. In this regard, however, it should be clarified that the headhunting aspect is not in any way related to their religion. Rather it is their form of capital punishment, related to our legalized methods of putting a condemned man to death via the hangman's noose or the gas chamber. It is at variance with our laws mainly in that a prisoner in the United States may petition for a new trial on the basis of additional evidence; in an aboriginal case, once one is pronounced guilty, the sentenced remains guilty!

With the Ifugaos, the verdict is based on supernatural laws and the use of divination and psychic help from the dead; often from the murdered man himself. A case in point is the following:

A short while before Ron and I arrived in the Ifugao area, a feud between two natives belonging to different villages ended in a killing. The body of the murdered man was immediately taken home, where it was placed before his *kubo* (thatched hut) in a sitting position supported by a wooden board.

For seven days the women of the family walked around the dead man, shouting heatedly that he take revenge on his assassin. One member of the family was missing, the deceased's wife, who had been taken to another *kubo* on the edge of the village to suffer the ordeal of a widow's mourning. Throughout the seven days of the dance, during which the women continued on in their shouts of insults and screams of vengeance, the wife sat in the same position as the corpse, covered by a blanket. And with the exception of infrequent drinks of water, she remained without food.

On the fateful seventh day, she was ceremoniously uncovered and led back to the body of her husband. The warriors of the village and other males related to the deceased dressed for a ritual dance

A tribal ceremony.

Ifugao triblesman playing his "nose-flute."

that preceded the burial ceremony. Reaching above their heads were cap-like affairs made of leafsheaths and betel-nut palm. These palms and leaves had been carefully picked from around the place where the killing took place, possibly to remind them that neither they nor the dead man could rest until revenge had been attained.

The burial dance started some distance from the village. With their wooden clappers and kettle drums they danced over trails and along the walls of the rice terraces until finally they came to a halt in front of the deceased's *kubo*. By now the warriors were worked up into a frenzied ecstasy; stopping before the widow they lifted the blanket from about her, and, taking her with them, they offered prayers to their deities to allow revenge to descend on the killer.

A large pig was then sacrificed and all feasted, including the widow, while squatting about in the form of a circle. Next a white chicken was brought within the circle and its head was lopped off; it was allowed to flop about, headless, until it came to a stop. While the decapitated chicken was flopping about, the local medicine man attempted communing with the spirits of the dead in a kind of native seance, and among those spirits that of the murdered man was conjured to give advice as to whom was to be selected among the warriors to give him vengeance.

The manifestation was answered by the flopping of the chicken when the dead bird came to a stop, pointing to one of the warriors. No other words were spoken; he knew immediately what his task was to be.

It having been thus conclusively set that avengement will be rendered, the week-dead body of the man was placed on an *adagan* (kind of stretcher) and then carried by four men to the burial cave, where again it was placed in a sitting position, the head now being supported by a stick and the whole corpse covered with a blanket. Someday, after it rots away, with the bones falling to the earth below, the skull will remain hanging on the stick.

The Ifugaos' apparent powers of psychical phenomena, combined with their belief in help from the spirits of the dead, were then used to find the wanted killer. Actually, by this time—once the law of the Ifugaos, coupled with these uncanny methods of finding the quarry, has placed its mark upon him, there is seldom much resistance left in the hunted man. The avengement was soon completed, and another head joined the tribe's collection.

I have noted that these natural psychic powers are frequently more commonly developed among primitive people, and that in some ways there seems a direct correlation between the submersion of such faculties and the degree of the claim on one's mind of busy civilization. Perhaps this accounts for the fact that sages like to pursue the development of their inner powers alone, or in silent monas-

Punta chief of the Ifugaos.

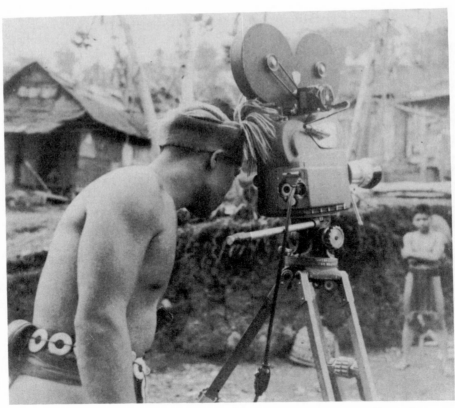

An Ifugao warrior examines our motion-picture equipment.

teries atop distant hills. One thing I do feel is that as these aborigines come more and more to be adopted into the hustling traffic of civilization, that which is natural to them now in special gifts of ESP could well be lost.

The hospitality we received from the Ifugaos was overwhelming. Somehow they sensed that our interests were sympathetic to their own, and a rapport was developed. Before long we were no longer looked upon as a novelty and were allowed full freedom of the area. That is when we photographed the cañao. We also asked to photograph some of the remains of human heads that had been collected, but this request they refused to grant, it being explained that to do so would take much away from the protective power of the talisman.

It is, I know, a repulsive matter to some people when the word "sacrifice" is used. The primitive people accept it with relish and it is an integral part of their life. Personally, it was a bit distasteful to Ron and myself, since we both hate to see any living thing killed. We discussed it at some length; unquestionably it does perform an important role in native occult practice. Indeed, sacrifices

Ifugao mummies seated upright in burial cave, Bontac area, Philippine Islands.

have been prominently featured throughout history as a factor in many religions. In India, today, certain Hindus offer daily sacrifices to their Goddess Calli, and, for that matter, so does our Bible disclose mention of sacrifices. In Leviticus 17:6 these words are spoken to Moses: "The priest must splash blood on the altar of Jehovah at the entrance of the trysting tent, burning the fat as a soothing odor to Jehovah."

I do not quote the above scripture to condone the primitive practice of the sacrifice, but merely to show how ancient such beliefs are. Mine is but the job of reporting the facts; I let the implications fall where they may. My personal interests lie more in the realm of investigating the psychical powers these native people seem to possess. Both Ron and I would like to learn more.

The next leg of the journey took us to Hong Kong where Ron Ormond wanted to film some of the religious practices of the Chinese, which have an atmosphere distinctly their own, unlike anything else in the world. We were fortunate; we arrived just in time to shoot the famous "Dragon Boat Races" (which I wrote about in *The Secret World of Witchcraft*), and the fabulous "Spirit Festival of the Cheung Chau Junkers," which is described in the next chapter.

IN HONG KONG

6

The Spirit Festival
of the Cheung Chau Junkers
of Hong Kong

Do the Chinese junkers have an instinct for danger at sea that out-does the best equipment of modern mariners? Does this race apart, who are born, live, and die upon the junks—those very seaworthy little boats that invest the China Coast—possess an uncanny weather-sense which may save their lives?

Inspector Paul Regan, Cheung Chau Island Police, observed a re-markable example of their abilities. One day a typhoon approached this small island in the vicinity of Hong Kong. Warnings were posted and the junks poured from the sea steadily into the harbor.

Then the typhoon, four hundred miles away, lulled, and the warnings were lowered. But the junks, who could see neither warn-ings nor typhoon while at sea, continued to seek safe berth.

Regan, in a police boat, was heading for Hong Kong. Suddenly the radio blared a warning. Imminent typhoon danger!

Regan yelled for throttle full ahead and arrived in port just as the typhoon hit. He barely made it, even with constant access to weather station reports. Yet the junkers, with neither radio nor help from scientific weather instruments, had started back to port hours before and had reached harbor well before him.

I questioned the Inspector about the junkers' sea instinct. Was it second sight, psychic ability, or some other faculty? He gave me little help. He simply said, "Whatever it is they have, it is sure something we don't have and it's bloody well accurate."

Inspector Paul Regan of the Cheung Chau Island Police, who made possible the filming of the Spirit Festival.

Investigation revealed, however, that the instinct has not always proved infallible. Marine Inspector George Watts of Cheung Chau told of a tragedy in 1937. A typhoon hit Hong Kong with 160 mile-per-hour winds. Ten thousand junkers were killed. Bodies were picked up out of the harbor for weeks afterwards.

I asked Watts what the Chinese thought of this incident.

"They merely philosophically stated, 'We had done evil, and the gods sought their vengeance. Life will now continue and it will not happen again.' I guess they were right, somehow, for it never did happen again, and the junkers have continued on in their uncanny mastery of the sea. You've got to hand it to those wily Chinese," Watts added with a crooked smile.

These stories greatly intrigued Ron and me, so we took police passage with these men direct to Cheung Chau, which lies close to the Mainland China coastline, some twelve miles east of Hong Kong, in what is known as Junk Bay. Because of its shape, Europeans have nicknamed it "Dumbell Island."

Camera and crew stand by, ready to shoot the beginning of the Cheung Chau Spirit Festival.

Cheung Chau is sacred ground to the junkers. It is their "home base," as it were, and here they congregate and for three fantastic days annually hold their fabulous Spirit Festival. There is nothing else quite like it to be found in the whole world, and yet, though it occurs but a mere twelve miles from a teeming metropolis, it is entirely unadvertised and is largely a private affair that tourists never see. For the Spirit Festival of Cheung Chau does not belong to the general masses of the busy Chinese who live in Hong Kong and on the mainland; it belongs to the junkers, and they are a people apart.

Cheung Chau at Spirit Festival time.

Yet, naturally, the British in authority on Cheung Chau know of it. It was these two well-groomed and ramrod-straight officials of the island, Chief Divisional Inspector George Watts and Inspector Paul Regan, who made our investigation of this ceremony possible. These men stood right by our side as Ron shot pictures and I took notes, while a myriad of firecrackers (some mighty big ones) popped by our feet. The firecrackers tossed at us, it was later explained, were not thrown in a spirit of malicious mischief; rather it was a deliberate attempt to scare away the evil spirits with which we, as occidentals, were supposed to be invested.

The Spirit Festival of Cheung Chau is held once each year, beginning on the sixth day of the fourth month of the Chinese calendar, which is roughly a month behind our own. For the three days of its celebration, junks of every size and description swarm in masses about this small sacred island.

Before the British began to administer Cheung Chau, and even for some time afterwards, the island was a notorious stronghold of Chinese pirates and smugglers. When, a good part of a century ago, some semblance of law and order was finally forced upon the reluctant inhabitants, more respectable people, finding themselves able to enjoy security under British protection, began to settle on the island, and it eventually became the headquarters of the junkers. During this period of development, many skeletons and remains of mutilated bodies were discovered as foundations for new houses were being excavated.

Here was evidence of atrocities that must be appeased. Every disaster that befell the new settler—be it sickness, bad luck, or persistent lack of prosperity—gradually came to be associated in the people's minds with the vengeful spirits of the unfortunates who had been tortured and murdered on the island during what has been dubbed "the bad old days" before the arrival of the British.

Eventually, the new inhabitants appealed to their Taoist priests to visit Cheung Chau and endeavor to find some way of pacifying the violent spirits which still roamed the island, wreaking their vengeance upon the contemporary population. The priests duly arrived and held council. As a result the *Ta Chiu,* or ghost-placating festival, now popularly called The Spirit Festival of Cheung Chau, was inaugurated. Each year since this highly colorful and symbolic ceremony has been faithfully observed.

Preparation for the festival begins some two months in advance of the opening day, when three acknowledged masters of the intricate art of papier-mache figure-making, familiar with every detail of costume and design, set to work fashioning effigies of the four principal deities who figure in the festival. These gods stand some nine feet in height and are gorgeously arrayed in all the traditional finery associated with their exalted status.

Three of the foursome are Shan Shaang, the red-faced god of the earth and mountains, To Tei Kung, god of the household, who reports good and evil, and Dai Sze Wong, corresponding to our own Devil, the god of Hades.

Seated between the horns that sprout from Dai Sze Wong's forehead is Kwan Yam, goddess of mercy, her presence there indicating the evil deity's inferiority to the forces of goodness. Dai Sze Wong also has a lieutenant in the person of the fourth god-figure, Hak Mo Sheung, which means "Black Mo Sheung," who stands a bit apart from the other three.

Black Mo Sheung is of Heaven, yet he is servant to the Devil God, his function being to discipline the evil people when they die as the evil spirit's mentor. Mo Sheung has twelve disciples who are his escorts, pygmy in size and dressed as soldiers, grouped about him.

These figures of the various Chinese gods related to the spirit

Figures representing the Chinese gods of Shan Shaang, To Tei Kung, and Dai Sze Wong preside over the Cheung Chau Spirit Festival.

Figure representation of the Chinese God, Hak Mo Sheung (Black Mo Sheung of Heaven), surrounded by his twelve pygmy-sized disciples.

festival, when completed, are mounted on pedestals, under appropriate palm-thatched shelters, on the opening day of the ceremonies.

In the evening of this opening day, precisely at midnight, saffron-robed Taoist priests solemnly read a citation to the junkers closely gathered about in a sardine-packed throng, recommending a vegetarian diet for the festival period, coupled with a variety of religious observances as tokens of homage to the gods, thereby encouraging the deities to ward off all evils, epidemics, and calamities during the coming year. A copy of the document is then placed in the hands of an effigy messenger, mounted on a paper steed, and is ceremoniously burned to speed him on his way to deliver the petition to the gods. Next the priests form a procession, in which the children impersonate adults and march through the entire area, reading aloud, again and again, the citation for everyone to hear.

It is regarded as essential to the success of the Spirit Festival of Cheung Chau that all of these preparatory proceedings be completed on the opening day. The main shrine is next erected, and the elaborate figures of the gods are mounted in their respective sheltered places of honor.

The ground to be used for the actual "spirit feast" is next carefully marked out; every path is arranged to lead to this all-important area, each being marked by a bamboo pole surmounted by a straw coolie hat and a paper lantern. At intervals, along the paths to the "spirit feast," are arranged small shrines of colored paper. Three times daily during the festival, a priest visits each of these shrines, placing before each three bowls of rice, three of tea, three of wine, and three of vegetables. The priest then burns joss-sticks and offers prayers, after which he removes all but four of the bowls. The bamboo poles along the paths are intended to mark the entry places for the wandering spirits, while the offering at the shrines serves to give them strength on their journey to the feast-ground.

An integral part of this opening ceremony is the donation of money for the purchase of buns especially baked for the occasion. These buns, or loaves of bread, are substantial affairs, four of them weighing one catty, the equivalent of one and a half pounds. The buns, when collected, are then affixed in hundreds to huge circular towers, somewhat resembling enormous industrial smokestacks, dotted about the area. The two largest of these erections measure some twenty-six feet in circumference at the base and rise to a height of approximately sixty feet. The buns each have a special red "chap" mark upon them, and those on the two largest towers bear a striking design of a dragon.

According to ancient custom, these buns attached to the towers must not be eaten, or even touched, before the spirits have had their complete fill on the final day of the festival. It is believed that anybody so underhanded as to steal one will be instantly seized with severe stomach cramps. Even during the grim days of the Japanese occupation, when people were very hungry, this prohibition was rigidly observed.

The second day of the Spirit Festival of Cheung Chau begins around eleven o'clock in the morning when five tables are set out in the form of a square, the fifth table being placed in the center. Mothers place their children's clothing on these tables; a form of pudding is also brought out, together with numerous lengths of yellow paper streamers. Six priests collect all of these items, and while

Joss-sticks are burned in reverence before the Chinese god-figures at the Spirit Festival.

carrying them commence an intricate march between and around the tables. This peculiar ceremony is named Tsau Ng Chi, which, interpreted literally, means "to run five times." By the end of two hours this ritual is complete; and the garments have in the process been stamped with a special mark inside the neckband of each article in the belief that such will overcome any misfortune from befalling the wearer during the ensuing year. The pudding is next eaten, and this, too, also protects one from ill health. The yellow streamers, which bear inscribed characters, are next hung on door lintels to safeguard the home from disaster. This beneficent ceremony is thus completed.

The afternoon of this second day finds the great parade ready to

The burning cage. Written prayers from the living are burned as messages sent to the spirits of loved ones who have departed.

take place. This is truly a spectacle to be seen. Each temple and village on the island is represented by its own throned deity. Accompanying the gods in the procession are the banner-bearers, waving their triangular-shaped flags of silk and vividly colored streamers inscribed with Chinese characters. It is a gorgeous sight as they move along. Music to the parade is provided by buffalo-skin drums, cymbals of all sizes, and Chinese flutes and horns. To our westernized ears, it was a blaring racket, but from the expressions on the faces of the junkers, it was obviously most satisfying.

Last came the real piece-de-resistance of the parade—the amazing tableaux, which are borne on long poles by perspiring coolies. These are truly remarkable. The characters are enacted by small children and depict various virtues and vices of mankind. All are dressed in

Nourishment for spirits. Gigantic towers of bread mount toward the sky as food for the dead.

Ron Ormond moves in for a close view at the base of the fabulous "Towers of Bread."

beautiful traditional costumes, but what makes the tableau so remarkable is the fact that one child may sit, stand, or kneel on the floor of the platform with another youngster apparently precariously balanced on his or her outstretched hand. To the uninitiated it must have appeared almost like magic. But, with inside "know-how" of conjuring, although Ron and I had no chance to actually examine the apparatus, we figured that it must have been accomplished by some clever arrangement of metal frames, harnesses, and wire. This is only a guess, of course. Actually, all we can say is that the whole arrangement is extraordinarily ingenious and effective.

The third day of The Spirit Festival follows more or less the same pattern as the second day. After the parade has wound its way through the village and around the paddy-fields, the performers take time out for refreshments, and the crowds drift back to the feast-ground. By this time, Dai Sze Wong, together with his helpful lieutenant, Hak Mo Sheung, and the latter's twelve soldier disciples, has been stationed at the end of the area which will later be occupied by the feast-tables. All who wish may donate food for this symbolic meal, and as every islander possesses ancestors who may possibly be present in a ghostly or spirit form, there is no shortage of good things to eat or drink. In addition, paper representations of money, boats, automobiles, and the many good things the invisible guests may have enjoyed or longed for in life are set out for their spirits' pleasure. It is truly a great occasion, especially for the ghosts, as no fewer than thirty-six lavishly supplied tables are laid for the spirits!

As the evening shadows begin to fall, joss-sticks, wax candles, rice-paper prayers, and imitation money are burned as offerings, and after dark the thousands of lighted joss-sticks stuck in the ground

Teeming throngs watch the Cheung Chau Spirit Festival parade.

The parade honoring the spirits of the dead continues on throughout the afternoon.

Striking tableaux of children, dressed in traditional costumes, are borne above the crowd, forming the great Cheung Chau Spirit Festival parade.

resemble countless fireflies, emitting plumes of scented smoke which pervade the whole atmosphere.

Now comes the veritable climax of the entire festival, "the snatching of the buns" from the gigantic towers. This event is greatly anticipated by all, and the crowd settles to wait with surprising patience through the long hours of the night until 2:30 in the morning.

As the appointed hour approaches, the tension begins to grow. A sort of nervous restlessness seems to seize on the patiently waiting crowd. Yet there were still no voices raised; just a nervous rustling was to be heard. Every person at the festival knows that he or she must remain sitting on the ground until a gong is struck as a signal from the high priest, who, by peering through a circular piece of precious jade, is able to witness the departure of the last spirit from the feast. He peers carefully about the whole area, using the jade much like we would a pair of binoculars. When he is sure that all the invisible guests are gone, he gives the signal.

With a "crash!" of the gong reverberating through the early morning hours, the mad scramble is on! Never had we seen such bedlam. The crowd literally seemed to spring up as one surging animal, and the buns began to melt away from the huge towers like magic. The ones lower down naturally went first to eager, plucking hands, while excited competitors tried to grab them from rivals who had already made their snatch. Scores of younger and more agile contestants swarmed up the towers from inside, smashing their way through the layers of bamboo frames in order to get the buns higher up. Once secured, these prizes were stuffed into their shirts and every available pocket, after which they tossed the remainders to the milling crowd below, the people scrambling madly for each flying bun as it descended. The shouting, the din, the maddening racket was indescribable.

Meanwhile, the women, in their own way, had been busy as, equipped with large baskets, each vied to outdo the other in scooping up quantities of the "goodies" heaped upon the spirits' banquet tables. Here was food for their respective households. Nothing was wasted, that is for sure; every scrap of that feast was made use of by scores of hungry souls.

In less than ten minutes after the striking of that gong, the gigantic towers were down, not a bun was to be seen, and the tables had been completely stripped.

With surprising quickness the crowds of people, tired but cheerful, melted away into the night leaving the area empty. The spirits had been duly placated for another year!

Ron and I stood gazing out over the now empty area. Something almost reverent hung over it; much like the stillness found inside

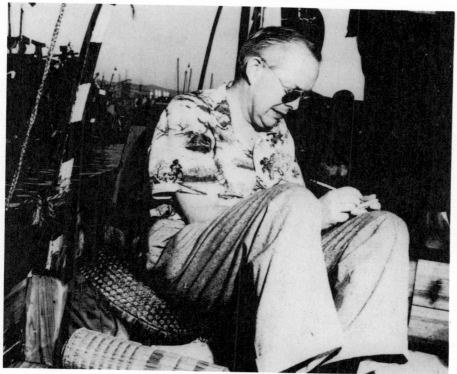

Ormond McGill on the job of constant on-the-spot reporting, covering the great religious mysteries of the Orient.

of a great cathedral. Had there really been spirits present at that feast for the dead?

We, as two lonely Americans on a journey to investigate the strange and unusual in these far-away places, honestly couldn't say. What we did know was that to the hundreds of people who attended that amazing festival, the spirits were most certainly there, as real to them as any tangible earthly thing.

It is all too easy to smugly scoff away all that does not fit into one's personal philosophy by saying, "It's nothing but superstition." But after all, the Chinese are a far older race than we are; maybe in the course of long centuries they have come to appreciate, as natural occurrence, that which we of the West only vaguely sense.

Somehow I felt a cold chill begin to tingle up my spine. I glanced at Ron. He glanced at me. We said nothing, and walked away, immersed in silence, contemplation, and memories of The Spirit Festival of the Cheung Chau Junkers.

We left Hong Kong for Taiwan; here further adventures awaited us among the Chinese. This was our first introduction to the venerable religion of Buddhism.

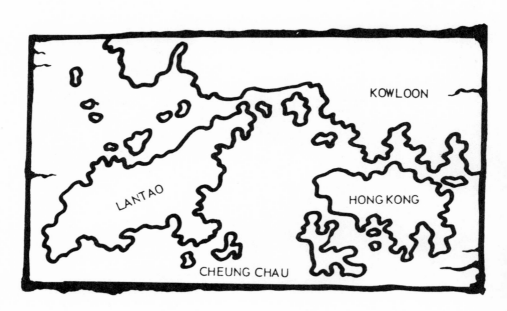

MAP OF HONG KONG-CHEUNG CHAU ARE.

IN TAIWAN

7

Some Buddhistic Insights from Taiwan

In mainland China there has existed for centuries one family whose members, generation after generation, have devoted themselves to the making of the figure of the Buddha. So deeply respected were these craftsmen by the Chinese, that when many people were forced to leave the mainland sanctuary and move to the Island of Formosa, now known as Taiwan, this family was officially escorted to the new Republic of China.

They have a unique process of constructing the figure of spun silk that makes the artifact amazingly light, yet at the same time, remarkably strong. It is then decorated in elegant style and trimmed in gold.

Since both Ron and I had a strong desire to bring back to America at least some religious treasures of the Orient, we sought one of these creations and were rewarded with a masterpiece which we sent to the States. Again our foresight in forming AOPSA had come to our aid. Before shipment, a special ceremony in the Buddhist abbotcy of Taipei was afforded the figure.

As the Chinese say, one picture speaks a thousand words, so I will let the pictures in this chapter tell the story of this dedication of the Buddha to world harmony and love between the people of East and West.

In the introduction to this book, I promised to tell further of The Red Swastika Society, as we found it in Taipei. In the next chapter I will keep that promise.

The shrine in the Buddhist abbotcy of Taiwan.

With the instructors of "The Eight-Fold Path" at the Buddhist abbotcy, Taipei, Taiwan.

The abbot prays that the Buddha may prove a symbol of world peace.

The Buddha we brought back to the United States.

The blessing of the Buddha for America.

A Buddhist precept. These precepts are object lessons. (Just as the Christians have their Ten Commandments, the Buddhists have their precepts of behavior for worthy living. These are frequently presented in symbolic paintings.) The Chinese have great respect for pictorial representation, feeling that pictures convey ideas more powerfully than words. This symbolic painting shows the sin of adultery, and the aftermath of torture undergone by the soul in the Buddhist "hell."

A Buddhist precept. This one illustrates the sin of drink and symbolizes the aftermath of torture undergone by the soul in the Buddhist "hell."

Rhythmic drumming is used to induce the mood of meditation within the abbotcy.

Ormond McGill and Ron Ormond with Buddhist nuns and monks at the Taiwan Abbotcy, Republic of China.

The state of meditation.

A Buddhist abbot wears the "AOPSA" insignia. Many religious leaders in the Orient have become members of the American organization.

8

The Red Swastika Society
of China

Next to their revered *True Gospel of God,* the sacred "Picture of God" is held in the greatest esteem by thousands of Chinese and members of The Red Swastika Society. The picture hangs above the altar in the shrine of the Holy-of-Holies of the Society. Its attainment is regarded as one of the most remarkable phenomena ever experienced by man. This description of that occurrence is taken directly from the official manual of The Red Swastika Society:

"The Spring Day, which falls every year around February 4th, has always been an important day in China. It marks the return of life when trees begin to open their new buds and all living beings have an urge to multiply themselves.

"For the Chinese and members of our Movement, it is a day set apart in memory and celebration of two of the most unusual events ever to happen in the entire history of mankind. One is the giving to the Chinese of *The True Gospel of God,* and the other is taking of the sacred "Picture of God"—when, for the first time, God allowed a photograph to be taken of Himself.

"This photograph was made on top of a famous mountain in Shantung, China, near Tasinan, known as the Mountain of a Thousand Buddhas, on November 21, 1921, and was witnessed by twenty-eight devotees of the Movement who had to climb up the mountain in bitter cold. It was taken by four men who received

111

specific instructions through the "Sand Board"[1] as to where and how to take it. The photographers did not see anything significant in the sky that day, which was rather cloudy, but following instructions precisely they left the camera open for a few seconds and when the film was duly developed, a figure with an old, dignified and benign mien appeared on it. This photograph is open to view today in the Mother Temple, as well as in several branch Temples."

As it was explained to Ron and myself, this photo-taking was a mere manifestation of Himself to his Chinese believers in a modern

---

1. "The Sand Board" is an oriental device used for spirit communication. It functions much like the well-known Ouija board of the west. The device consists of a board upon which a layer of sand is spread, then the medium and devotee combine in grasping a forked stick and suspending it over the "Board;" as the spirit takes control the stick dips and moves about in the sand leaving its mark thereupon. The message is then read, or interpreted, as the case may be. This process is especially effective when applied to Chinese characters, as the nature of their writing is to convey meaning in expression of line strokes.

Throughout the Orient, in connection with its variety of religions, belief in spirits is frequently held. Not only in the spirits of the dead, but in connection with what oriental people refer to as "The High Spirits," Associates of God, and even of God, Himself. God to them is an extremely real being, who, far from being regarded as something remote and distant, is very definitely a personality vitally interested in each of His many children, and He is willing and able to directly communicate with each when the proper methods of devotion are applied.

Ron and I saw this direct communication with God among the Chinese in Manila, the Taoists in Hong Kong, the Buddhists in Taiwan, Burma, Thailand, and the Caodaists of Vietnam, about which I will write in the next chapter. Their explanation of such direct communications with God is remarkably logical. Here are the words of a student in this regard:

"I have been a devout person all my life and believe in and practice prayers. I now feel that prayers of this nature, as performed by so many people of the Occident, are 'one way traffic.' We send our supplications to the Lord in words or thoughts but give Him no opportunity to pour His spirit back to us. Through my religious studies in the Orient with Caodai and its accompanying phenomena of direct communication with Divine Spirits, I now understand more clearly why Jesus often went up to a hill and communed with God for long periods of time either by Himself or with His disciples."

The "Signature of God" in Chinese, exactly as it appears signing all messages received on the "sand-board" from the Almighty. The "signature" has been formed into gigantic plaques decorating the walls of The Red Swastika Society's shrines.

way according to the official manual, which continues, "In the old days, God revealed Himself several times to Abraham, Moses, and the other prophets and holy men."

It was with the special sanction of the Society that we were permitted to bring back a copy of this "Picture of God" to show to the people of the Occident. Ron took a photograph of it as it hung over the altar of the Red Swastika Society in Taipei. He tried in vain to bring it into sharp focus, but as the original was in soft definition it was impossible to render it otherwise than here shown.

We have often speculated about this picture. Is it but some unusual cloud formation that was recorded on film? Strangely, it seems much too definite in form and completeness to be just that. Also, somehow, it seems most appropriate that God would manifest in the "appearance" of the people to which He reveals Himself, which He assuredly did in this photograph.

In this picture, Ron and I fulfill a trust that was placed upon us and present it with the deepest of respect. The reader is asked to remember that this "Picture of God" is an object of great reverence to thousands of people in China.

Shrine of The Red Swastika Society in Taipei, Taiwan. Note "The Picture of God" which hangs above the altar.

The Chinese "Picture of God." This sacred photograph is revered by thousands of Chinese in mainland China, Hong Kong, and Taiwan.

IN VIETNAM

9

Caodaism and the
White Brotherhood in Vietnam

Ron and I visited and met with the Cardinals of Caodai together. Subsequently, following our experiences in India, Ron had the opportunity to again visit the Holy City and was admitted into The White Brotherhood. He writes this report of adventures with these fascinating and devout people.

———————

The huge Caodai temple drum boomed twice. I struck a match to glance at my wrist watch; it was 2:00 a.m. Every hour around the clock the drum had resounded out the time, like the wailing of a lost soul from some cavernous depth. Somehow you got the feeling of remote loneliness, and yet, strangely, it was equally warm and hospitable.

I had been lying in my cot staring blankly at the ceiling; now I rose quietly, slid into my sarong-like *sham* pants, opened the door and slipped out into the humid Vietnamese night. I had scarcely reached the street when I heard the soft paddle of feet behind me. I turned toward the sound and noted Phan-Tai-Doan, the interpreter assigned to me by the administrative body of the Holy City, following a few steps behind me.

"Our new brother is nervous, or could it be that he is excited tonight?" he asked gently.

"Perhaps a little excited," I countered as we walked along.

"And no wonder, for it is not often that another member is taken into the Caodaist White Brotherhood."

119

Outside views of *"The Holy See of Caodai."* This structure was also shown in The Secret World of Witchcraft, *which is the companion to this book. These two books present "both sides of the coin," witchcraft, the negative (evil) aspect of worship, and religion the positive (good).*

"How many other white men have become brothers in the order," I inquired further.

"You are one of the very few to be so honored by the Caodaists."

"I am deeply moved," I said, significantly.

"Where would our brother be going now—to the Grand Temple?"

"No," I rejoined simply. "I go to the small temple where the Christian Jesus is seated among the other sages of the East."

"Good, then I will join you in your prayers."

The small temple I had referred to was one situated not far from the Grand Temple of Caodai itself. High above the altar, in the typical and ornate manner of oriental drawings, was a picture simultaneously showing Buddha, Confucius, Mohammed, Lao-Tze, and other Masters. But most startling of all was the representation of Jesus the Christ as He sat among the other Sages.

As we walked toward the small temple, I recalled the details that had led me to this meeting with the Caodaists, a meeting which had been dramatically climaxed by my initiation into the White Brotherhood. Before that, I had gone to Vietnam with my partner in adventure, Ormond McGill. We both had done a comparatively thorough job of research, and the information we obtained was thrilling.

The call to worship.

The spectacular "Midnight Mass of Caodai," within The Holy
See.

Caodaism, while less than fifty years old, has grown to a membership of more than three million adherents, with some four hundred churches and over two thousand missionaries. The Holy City, located at Tayninh, Vietnam, has grown to a population of over ten thousand devotees, has its own schools, markets, hospitals, farms and administration buildings, and is beautifully landscaped with modern grounds and streets. In addition, it boasts the only college that specializes not only in teaching oriental philosophy and comparative religions but in the opening of "the third eye" via the art of meditation.

The first time I went to the Holy City with Mac, we had heard rumors of the order's beginning and wanted to check them further. Accordingly, we found Caodaism was born of spiritism in 1925 by a group of Vietnamese scholars, who by dabbling in divine (automatic) writing, had received surprisingly good results. We wanted to confirm this report ourselves, so when we were ushered into the office of

Caodaist students at "The College of Third-eye Vision," learning the art of meditation. Conservatory of Caodaism, Holy City of Tayninh, Vietnam.

the legislative body, which also served as the dwelling establishment of the three administrative cardinals, we inquired into this aspect of Caodaism.

"What is there so surprising or unexpected in the spiritist origins?" As Cardinal Le-Thein-Phuoc admirably put it, "True, some have tried to clothe off by ridicule divine message transmitted by the turning of tables, billed baskets, or oracles from a medium. But it should not be regarded as more surprising or unexpected in using such vehicles than is the Divine Power making Itself heard on a Sinai surrounded with lightning and thunder."

So saying, he dropped into silence and looked toward us expectantly. We could do no more than nod our appreciation of his words. The entire conversation was conducted in Vietnamese, as neither Le-Thein-Phuoc or his two fellow cardinals spoke a word of English. Fortunately, we had the services of a most able interpreter, whose smooth fluency allowed us a freedom of questions and answers.

As we pondered the cardinal's words, we could not help but agree that he had a point well taken, for the idea of spirit communication with God and His associated divine hosts is not nearly as foreign to other religious movements as, at first thought, it might appear. Nearly every religion has as its source some divine revelation that appeared, or "came through," to some person. These revelations are the very essence of their beginning. Christianity, for example, is full of references to experiences where God manifested Himself and directly communicated with man, or else allowed the communication of His associated spirits (or angels) with mankind.

The Caodaists have merely come to hold that these miraculous communions with God need not necessarily be a rarity, and use the power of communion regularly, in what they refer to as "The Cell of Meditation," for the direction of church activities, and through the church, the direction of the lives of their members. To them, God is a very personalized deity who is vitally filled with compassionate love for *all* His children. He is considered as the One God, regardless of the many and diverse names by which He may be called. To the Jews, He is known as Jehovah; to the Moslems, He is known as Allah; to many others, He is simply God; but to the Caodaists, He is called Cao-Dai, which simply means Cao (high) and Dai (palace). Literally speaking, then, the Supreme Palace (place) where reigns the Almighty.

Even in their representation of God, the Caodaists have shown wisdom, for He is not shown in human form.

"As such," another one of the cardinals, Nguyen-Trung-Hau, put it, "He would not be suited for universality and understanding, as each people has its own vanity. Instead, we represent Him as He

A nun of Caodai.

prescribed He should be shown, simply by an "eye" which is the symbol of the Universal Conscience and the individual conscience."

I glanced at McGill as he shot a question.

"Is it a symbol of 'the third eye,' as is mentioned by the lamas of Tibet?"

"When the Universal Conscience and the individual conscience

"The All-Seeing Eye of God," official symbol of the Caodai
religion. This motif is repeatedly used in their architecture.

are one, then you have third eye vision. Your mentioning of Tibet
is interesting since The White Brotherhood of Caodai and The
White Brotherhood of Tibet are in close communication."

"Communication!" we both almost shouted, stunned!

"Yes, communication by way of the mind as we experience it in
meditation."

We were, to say the least, impressed, but there still remained
facets of their belief that might prove difficult for many people of
the West to comprehend. The Caodaist faith shows five great *way-
showers*: 1. Jesus the Christ; 2. Buddha, the communicator; 3. Confucius, the educator; 4. Lao-Tze, the philosopher, and - 5. The Ascended Masters, who constitute the occult August Hierarchy of the
Caodaists.

The combining into one of all forms of religion, such as the elements of spiritism, oriental philosophy, and Buddhistic conceptions of *going within,* along with the spiritual principles of Christianity, may indeed be difficult for many occidentals, who are used to recognizing their own special form of worship as the only path to God, to accept. But I would feel remiss in my duties if I did not add that in this unique combination there is a spirit of democracy and tolerance, a uniting of good people of all faiths in a common bond of understanding that is worthy of consideration.

Any religion, despite its variations or organization and/or method of worship, must stand or fall on one simple value, its philosophy of life, not only for the creed's sake but for its members, and, it might be included, for all peoples of the world.

For a better understanding of Caodaism, let us consider one of its tenets:

Light comes only from light. The light here proceeds from the light above. Human light, then, proceeds from divine light which shines on all people, irrespective of color or race, belief or religion; thus, all men and women are in reality brothers and sisters: so lend aid in the cause of human brotherhood and be kind to one's neighbors. Be also kind toward animals, and of plants, too, see that they are treated well, for all life is of God.

Here was something truly worthy for any religion to follow and be rightfully proud of. I turned to my partner, who nodded significantly.

"Any other questions?" I asked him.

"Perhaps we should inquire into their methods of communication with God."

I leaned over toward our interpreter to put the question to him, but it was not necessary. The cardinals either sensed or read our minds.

One of the cardinals put it directly: "We Caodaists believe, in common with some Christians, that it is possible to have direct communication with God and his high saints, spirits, or angels. Of course, some beliefs relegate such communion to areas of the past and no longer regard it as possible in modern times. We maintain that it is still possible and make a regular practice of doing so . . ."

I glanced in the direction of McGill, who at the moment seemed completely fascinated at what he had just heard. "Kind of like the belief that Joseph Smith founded the Church of the Latterday Saints on," he stated.

I remembered the account from having previously read of the origin of the Mormons, namely, "While I was thus in the act of

Monks of Caodai.

Ron Ormond with officials of The White Brotherhood.

calling upon God," Joseph Smith wrote, "I discovered a light appearing in the room, which continued to increase until the room was lighter than at noonday. . . ."

It was this that prompted my next question.

"Where are these communions held?"

"In a very sacred building," Cardinal Thruong-Van-Trang furnished, "in a secret chamber called 'The Cell of Meditation.' It is here that many of our Divine Communions take place."

It was during my return trip to the Holy City that I had the unique experience of entering the sacred "Cell of Meditation." I had somehow expected the place to be sumptuously furnished with thick rugs and overstuffed couches. Here, however, the only furnishings that were in evidence were a bed with a polished wood surface for a mattress and a small table on which stood a huge bowl of fresh fruit. The cell had no windows. Even so, the room did not seem dark, and one hardly had to speak above a whisper to be heard; speaking in such a room seemed almost superfluous.

There was a "feeling" about the room that is very difficult to explain. I have spent days in oriental monasteries and am quite used to the feeling of aloneness, but this room was quite different. On first entry, it gave me a sensation of vertigo, as though I stood on the threshold of the cosmos. Then quickly it was gone. This is the only way I can express it. In all of my life, I have never been in such a room, and it was only because of my acceptance into The White Brotherhood of Caodai that I was permitted entrance on this occasion.

During the period I remained at the Holy City on my second trek, I made every effort to probe into their religion, and I must add, at no time did they attempt to hold back details. During these sessions they told me why they remained strict vegetarians, showed me the disposition of their altar and the meaning of every item thereon, their methods of meditation, of prayer, and other particulars about their philosophy.

It was about 2:15 a.m. when Phan-Tai-Doan and I entered the small temple with the unusual picture of Jesus seated among the other masters of the mysterious Far East. As is their custom, only one candle burned in the room, but the picture seemed alive with brilliance. I studied it carefully, noting every detail in the faces of all: Jesus the Christ, Buddha, Confucius, Lao-Tze, Mohammed. Somehow it seemed quite natural and appropriate for them all to be thus together. It occurred to me that here, indeed, was a most excellent example of the broad tolerance that I had often heard preached but seldom seen. I recalled the words of Cardinal Thruong-Van-Trang: "A place where a believer or unbeliever may lift up his soul towards a hope of predilection by worshipping Jesus

The inner shrine. Holy of Holies of Caodai, showing the great symbolic sphere, representative of the universe, with the all-seeing "Eye of God" at its center.

Christ, by venerating Gautama Buddha, by admiring Confucius, or by seeking wisdom from the Ascended Masters."

Both Phan-Tai-Doan and I knelt on the floor to pray. I said the Lord's Prayer, while he prayed in Vietnamese. When we finished he said quietly, "Over fifty thousand hours of prayer have been said in this room beneath that picture; that is why the picture is so sacred."

Afterward, as we returned to our rooms, both the interpreter and I were strangely quiet. Words were hardly necessary at a time like this. When I turned to enter my room, Phan-Tai-Doan smilingly said, "You will sleep well now." I nodded agreement and closed the door behind me to enjoy, as he had predicted, one of the best night's sleep of my life. But even so, my awakening was even more dramatic, for propped against the wall was the unique and unusual picture of Jesus and the other masters.

At first, I was dumbfounded, thinking it was only an illusion, but to my pleasant surprise it was the real picture, which had been presented to me as a gift by Cardinal Thruong-Van-Trang. Ormond McGill and I have proudly used it as the frontispiece to this book.

When I left the Holy City, I did so with regret, for never had I been treated more understandingly, or with more respect. I felt a great new appreciation for my oriental brothers and for the religion of Caodaism. With me I brought, in addition to the venerated picture I have mentioned, a most wonderful book, titled "The Master Way," based on the teachings of the Masters of the East. It is one of the greatest books of ancient wisdom and philosophy it has been my good fortune to study.

I am happy to report, my partner shares these views with me.

Faith seems to be an ingredient universal to all religions worldwide. Caodaism being a religion encompassing such a variety of faiths, our journey seemed an excellent opportunity to learn more of this important subject. We spoke to the cardinals of Caodai at length. The gist of their comments are in the next chapter.

10

The Power of Faith of Caodai

The greatest power in all the world is faith. It is man's heritage of divinity; it is his *key* to unlocking the miraculous powers of the God-source. It has been said that with faith nothing becomes impossible.

There is a strong philosophy in the above, for with strong faith man can reach through to his inner self and call upon undreamed-of reservoirs of strength—the literal source of the power that works miracles.

During the ministry of Jesus Christ, when He sent forth his disciples to heal the sick, many of them returned depressed and called themselves failures.

"But why, Master," they pleaded, "why cannot we also perform miracles as you do; why cannot we so cure the sick and heal the suffering?"

Jesus's answer to his disciples was brief, and in it is the clue not only to the solving of their problem, but also to the all-encompassing power of this greatest of God-given gifts: "Because of your unbelief; for verily I say unto you, if ye have faith as a grain of mustard seed, ye shall say unto that mountain, 'Remove hence to yonder place,' and it shall remove and nothing shall be impossible unto you." Matt. 17:20.

Since man has this great heritage of power within himself to accomplish all things, how then account for failure? One thing and one thing only is the downfall. Unbelief. Unbelief in one's self, unbelief in one's own divine power, unbelief in the power of God to always bring success, health, love, and a life full of all that is good. For the power of faith is boundless; it ranges from the realm of

132

miracles to the most menial of accomplishments. It is a power held by all men, its power functioning in direct ratio to the square of one's belief. As the Master Jesus expressed it, "With faith greater things than I shall ye do."

We of Caodai state that the student must first come to appreciate the vast importance of cultivating this power of faith, and make it a positive factor in his life. To our students, we express that one must learn the principals of the inner power of the mind. And what is Mind? Mind, in its essential sense, is the higher element of the soul. And faith is thus seen as a function of the human soul, mind-faith being actually the study of God. And for the mastery of the study, the student must apply himself every bit as diligently as does the student of the professions. He must come to completely understand his subject and learn the rules of its operation. Here is a first rule of importance: Nothing can be promised to half-hearted service, or to a faith that is divided between good and evil, or between mind and matter.

"That is deep philosophy; we will try and explain," spoke one of the cardinals.

In the Orient, one holy man put the point of faith thus: "Be steadfast to principle, especially in the face of oppositions of sense and material possessions. If you have faith, and your cause is just and right, it will be as persistent as the shining of the sun upon a block of ice; soon its radiance overcomes the ice's coldness and hardness, and reduces it to its original substance." In other words, all one's faith must be placed in the Omnipotent One, and used toward the ends of good. So directed, faith becomes strongly charged with God-power. To quote:

"Since God is Good
And Life is Good,
Therefore God is Life,
And life is God."

To use faith toward evil ends is to pervert its power and invariably leads to eventual disaster. Just know that throughout all Gospels, whether they be Christian, Hindu, Buddhist, or Islamic, the preachments have forever been the same: "Choose ye this day whom ye shall serve."

Thus, the application of this first rule in the successful use of the power of faith in one's own life is to direct it toward that which is good: good as an objective reality, good both personally and altruistically to all mankind. So directed, the release of its power is clean and fine.

Look upon mind as the creative force and matter as the gross material that may be molded by mind for either good or evil. Faith is the methodology of releasing the power of God, while good may be regarded as the term defining the directing of mind toward the proper ends for the Godly-purposeful releasing of the power.

The second great rule for utilizing the power of faith is found herein: Do not seek all things, seek only in moderation. As the Buddha expressed it, "Follow the middle path." For example, to want material things as the needs of a happy life is good. But, to want material things as an end unto themselves is opposed to good. As an illustration, if a man owns a comfortable home, it should be used toward its end of providing love and pleasant living. But to want the possession of many homes, just for the purpose of possession or to show superiority over others is a distortion of the purposeful use of the power of faith, and hence is an evil end. The student must realize that the basic source of the power of faith is the Infinite One, and, at the same time, have faith that the Infinite One, simultaneously with providing the power, will direct him to the proper moderation of all things—down the middle path of the Buddha.

Come to look upon faith as a firm, persistent, determined belief in the Almighty Good; changeless, deathless, substantial Spirit as The All in All. Faith is the substance of everything you desire. Out of your own belief—be it directed toward that which is good—shall come that for which you are wishing. For faith means simply unswerving belief, and belief sets into operation those forces of God that can bring to man all that he shall ever need and purposefully desire.

All of the great masters have understood the operation of the power of faith. It was superbly demonstrated throughout the teaching of Jesus. He had complete understanding of the laws of the mind—and faith; one has only to recall His teachings to appreciate how basic it was to the performance of all of His miracles.

"Do you have *faith*?" He asked the lepers.

"We have *faith*, Master."

"Be ye healed!"

And they were healed.

Mark 11:22 sums it up in its entirety: "Have the faith of God."

We have stated that faith is believing. And what is believing? Is it, by way of example, believing in the power of Jesus Christ? Yes, if you are a Christian, that is one way of its expression. Is it believing in a certain creed? Not necessarily, as creeds tend to be antiquatedly dogmatic. Rather than creed, *belief in your belief* is the better expression. Believe in your own divinity even as Jesus believed in His. Believe in the God within you, just as Jesus believed in His Eternal Father—the One God in Him.

He who would see the mountains move at his word, who would

see loaves and fishes increase, and waters firm under his feet, and winds obey his word, must not have one doubt in his heart of his divine power, and realize that when he speaks that it is God speaking. With such unshakable belief, then, indeed, shall he who so believes have all his wants administered to—for he lets the Almighty speak the word—and through that faith everything shall be provided.

It will do well here to review a few famous historical incidents of those who have utilized faith.

Daniel in the Lion's Den is a splendid example, in which a man in dire danger called upon the power of faith—the God power—and came through the ordeal unscathed. The Biblical story of Jonah and the Whale is yet another.

Other examples of the power of faith come down history's long corridors.

Who taught Joan of Arc the art of warfare? How did Galileo and Kepler discover the "music of the spheres?" How did Homer learn to compose and sing heroic poems some two hundred years before the Greeks had an alphabet? Who taught Lincoln statesmanship? From whence came Benjamin Franklin's inspirations as a philosopher and inventor, or Isaac Newton's advanced learning as a mathematician and scientist?

Each of these greats found their way to the mighty reservoir of universal knowledge. They searched their inner selves and made an acquaintance with the God power and appropriated its treasures. In plainer words, they tapped the divine source of the soul wherein lies all knowledge—the knowledge of the ages—waiting, wondering who will be the next to dip into its mighty fount for the answers to all problems.

You know now of this secret place; each man must enter for himself and eat of the fruit from the tree of knowledge. The only payment is faith in God and faith in yourself as a divine being.

> Seek not with an anxious look,
> Quiet your worried mind,
> Know these words are true indeed,
> Seek and you must find.

In India, the Hindus recognize this unity of life, the divine individual selfhood, responding through vibrations with creative energy and the oneness of spirit that illuminates the soul. While it is not our intention to go into nomenclatures, we should try to make clear the use of the word, "soul." Here is the definition as given by many of the great sages of the Far East and India: Soul: our super-self, through which there are many ways to enter if we wish to grow and unfold spiritually. Man's individuality is determined by the endowments of his soul. The endowments of every soul are powers, faculties, and capacities: To know, to feel, to choose, and to designate these capacities as the intellect, the sensibility, and the will.

The Soul, ever enduring, ever enlarging, is the immortal but changing plane of the Entity (Super-self). Within *Itself* memory sits, the emotions repose, the imagination rises, and will and purpose find their enthronement. The Soul is dormant to conscious mind unless illuminated by Spirit. Spirit is the light of the Soul. Spirit is God. Spirit is universal. By It is man bound to the entire cosmos; through It he recognizes his divinity—his oneness with God, the creative essence, energy and force of the universe.

Another law of faith, then, is discovery. Long ago Emerson wrote, "God enters by a private door into every individual." But many of us do not have the remotest idea as to what is meant by God; neither do we know the way to the "private door," so this acceptance has brought us nothing. Then, through the darkness, there has come upon us a gradual revealing of the truth from the unknown. Such truths were not accepted conclusions from an established philosophy; rather they were truths which seemed to be forced upon the intellect. We, in Caodai, seemed to find a stream of knowledge sweeping around us whose course and source were undiscovered and unexplored. Mystified, we called it occultism and included under that mystic head a world of phenomena and thought which modern philosophy had not yet classified. Thinking men and women began to enter these dark portals, some in search of one demonstration, some another. Within these dim corridors the story of faith is learned, and now as it breaks on us in brightness, we are declaring occultism shall be occultism no longer, and the light that scatters the darkness is truth.

Now we know how blindly men have worked; how they have been led without ever discovering their leadership. We know how they might have freed their paths from hundreds of barriers on their way; that is, had they only recognized that the power of faith led to self-awareness, the inner self, the divinity of man and his oneness with God.

In considering the paraphilosophy of faith, we say it is well for the student to understand what is the best attitude of mind to maintain to receive the greatest blessings of good in the easiest way and in the shortest possible time. In this regard, it would be wise for some of us, as thinking adults, to observe the child and emulate his ways, viz.: a child needs, and must have love from his parents. When that love is expressed the child develops an unbounded faith in his parents. Such is the faith and the love that we must expect from the Divine Spirit. A child is plastic and ever eager to explore and seek out new ideas. Many of us make the mistake of growing up and developing set habits, dogmatic thoughts that we cling to with unreasoning tenacity. Question yourself; if you are one such person, then it is important that you become once again as the little child and make yourself eager and willing to learn. Sit calmly and quietly as the magistrate does, and listen with impartiality and without fear to the counsel of your "inner voice." You will find it there in meditation. You need not feel obligated to accept it given you thus, but have faith in your divine selfhood to adjust all things.

Always know, faith in God is truth. Love the truth and you love God. Know yourself and you know God. You don't ever have to be discouraged if there are times when everything seems to go wrong. In such times, study the lesson of faith and you will be surprised how lifted you feel. For faith is a powerful force, both faith in your Inner-self and faith in God. In moments of stress repeat these words of self-awareness:

> I am divine, not mortal,
> I am holy, not sinful,
> I am wise, strong, purposeful,
> I am what I am and I can do all things.

A wise guru once said: "It is not enough to listen to teachings alone; they must be put into practice." As we know in the learning of music, one who listens only to the theories and does not apply them will not become proficient. So it is with your application of using the power of faith. You must come to live the principles every day, every hour, every moment; thinking good and Godly thoughts. If one hears and learns of the rules, the laws, the lessons, that is but the beginning. If practice follows, you will have built your house upon rock and no matter how you may be assailed naught can prevail against you. You will stand, and the more storms beat about your house the more secure you will feel yourself within.

And, conversely, heed the warning: if you hear only and do not do, regardless of how great your learning, your wealth, or your position, you will be undermined by disaster.

We express it again: build faith upon a rock by continual application and practice. Believe in your omnipotence with God, through which all things become possible unto you.

And so accept these thoughts from the Masters:

"I am the thought of God, the idea of the Divine Mind. In Him I live, I move, I have my being. I am spiritual, harmonious, fearless and free. I am governed by the law of the universe—no more no less—the law of everlasting God, and all other laws are subservient to that law.

"I know the truth and the truth makes me free, for I have faith which frees me from all evil and from material bondage.

"God works through me to will and do whatever is to be done by me. I am happy. I am holy. I am loving. I am wise. I and the Father are one, because I have . . .
FAITH, FAITH, FAITH, FAITH, FAITH, FAITH, FAITH, FAITH, FAITH, FAITH."

So concludes this dissertation on faith by the Cardinals of Caodai. Through these insights we have a good glimpse into the heart of their beliefs, and through their beliefs a glimpse yet further into the major religions of the Orient.

They were wise men, these Cardinals of Caodai; it is well they had such faith, for they have suffered, as is frequently man's lot upon this earth. For the Holy City of Tayninh was eventually razed by the Vietcong during the long and tragic war in Vietnam. However, Caodai, like the proverbial phoenix, ever rises from the ashes.

From Vietnam, Ron and I proceeded on our journey. We were headed for Thailand. En route we made a stopover at one of the most mysterious spots on earth, legendary Angkor Wat in Cambodia.

The call to worship within the fabulous "Holy See" of Caodai.

IN CAMBODIA

11

Cambodia's Magnificent Monument to the Great Religious Mysteries of the Orient

The religions that are responsible for the building of Angkor and all the remarkable structures that are found in this remote area in the heart of the jungle regions of Cambodia are those of the ancient Khmer, which originated in the distant past of India.

About the year 1000 B.C., the Aryan tribes from the plains of Persia began to pour down towards India, bringing with them advanced religious conceptions of Vedas, or belief in a universal God, with, as its manifestations, a series of divine beings who ruled the physical phenomena of the world. Through their concepts and secret teachings, man could, by profound concentration, discover within himself hidden springs of forces and powers through which he could become master of all he surveyed; from this was born the habit of asceticism and retreat into isolated places to develop these faculties. This is the concept that resulted in mysterious Angkor being built in its remote region. What secrets were learned and studied there; what esoteric skills were learned, what forces unleashed? How indeed, were the very structures themselves raised in this isolated region those many centuries ago?

Occultists say these "miracles" were performed by powers of levitation wielded by the ancients. They speak of these as being the same forces used by the master race who built the Great Pyramid of Giza to lift gigantic blocks of stone into place, and the same mysterious powers that placed the Great Stone Faces of Easter Island

Angkor Wat, religious center of the vanished Khmers.

The grand gateway to the lost city of Angkor Thom, capital of a vanished civilization.

ever peering seaward. Pure speculation, of course, but most intriguing to conjecture upon. The structures of Angkor are in many ways the most remarkable of all, because the blocks of stone used are not only of tremendous size but are intricate beyond belief in construction and design.

There is something eerie about Angkor that one "feels" through channels other than the normal senses. Something that speaks deep within the very heart of the mind, a call to the innermost depths of being. One has but to open up one's mind and let the psychometry of the past flow in to feel in Angkor one of the great marvels of all the ages. If only those venerable walls could speak, what tales of wonder they could tell.

Harken, for they do speak; not with the physical voice of man, but with the inner voice of the spirit.

The remains of once all-glorious Angkor lie in the jungles to the north of the great lake, Tonle-Sap, the most conspicuous being the capitol of Angkor Thom and the temple of Angkor Wat, both of which are situated on the right bank of the river Siem-Reap, a tributary of the Tonle-Sap. Other remains of the same character lie scattered about the vicinity on both sides of the river. The grand city of Angkor is enclosed within a rectangular wall of stone nearly two miles long in each direction, which is entered by five monumental gates. Here are found the remains of palaces and temples, overgrown by the tropical forests. The chief of these are: 1. The vestiges of the royal palace and the pyramidal religious structure known as the Phimeanakas, both of which stand within an enclosure, to the east of which extends a terrace with magnificent reliefs. 2. The Temple of Bayon, consisting of a double system of galleries enclosing a cruciform structure, at the center of which rises a huge tower with a circular base. Fifty towers decorated with quadruple faces of Brahma are built at intervals upon the galleries, the whole temple ranking as perhaps the most remarkable of the Khmer remains.

Angkor Wat, the best preserved example of the Khmer's miraculous architecture, lies less than a mile to the south of the royal city, within a park surrounded by a moat, the outer perimeter of which measures 6,060 yards. This structure was devoted entirely to worship and formed a center of religious and esoteric learning. It consists of three stages, connected by exterior staircases which decrease in dimension as they rise, culminating in the sanctuary—a great central tower pyramidal in form. Three galleries with vaulting supported on columns lead from the three western portals to the second stage. They are connected by a transverse gallery, thus forming four square basins.

All of the structures are amazingly decorated with Khmer sym-

Mute faces, representative of the great god Siva, stare from the towers of Angkor Thom: If they could but speak, what wonders they could tell.

The temple of Bayon.

bolic patterns, profuse but harmonious, consisting chiefly in the representation of gods, men, and animals. Floral decorations are also seen, used mainly for borders, moulding, and capitals beautifully carved in huge blocks of sandstone which are placed together so accurately that they have withstood the ravages of the centuries.

As one stands in awe before the fabulous structures, the question surges into mind, "What happened to this great civilization that raised these tremendous edifices in the midst of wilderness and then vanished?"[1]. The Khmers have vanished, yet they have left behind a truly magnificent monument to the great religious mysteries of the Orient.

Our scheduled flight from Cambodia to Bangkok was ready to proceed, but since Ron wanted to do a bit more filming at Angkor Thom we decided to part ways for a short while. I flew on to Thailand to meet Harold Young at Chiengmai. Mr. Young was intimately acquainted with the hill tribes of the Lahu, about whom I will report in the next chapter.

While at the airport in Cambodia, it was a pleasant surprise to see veteran explorer Lowell Thomas step from the plane. He was there to arrange some footage for his television series. We chatted a bit, and I told him of Ron Ormond being in the area. Later the two men met and discussed their respective activities at Angkor Thom.

Ron rejoined me in Chiengmai, where I had written of the intimate relationship between religion and medicine among primitive people, and how the Lahu medicine men cure the sick with the use of herbs.

---

1. As I wrote in the chapter dealing with this subject in *The Secret World of Witchcraft,* occultists have a number of theories, one being that races of people, cycle after cycle, in the world's history rise to a peak of their usefulness on this planet, and, having fulfilled their purpose, pass on to a higher plane. Others, with more science-fiction learning, say that Angkor is one of the rare spots on Earth where there exists a gateway between dimensions—a "thin spot" in the vibrations of matter separating planes of existences. And through the advanced learning of the hidden secrets of nature by the ancients, the gateway was opened, leading a path to a parallel world through which the people passed to literally vanish from the face of the Earth.

There is yet another theory with a science-fiction touch that is popular. This belief is that the creation of Angkor, along with many other mysterious places of bygone ages, are the work of beings from distant planets who visited earth in the remote past. Having completed their work through superior scientific knowledge, these visitors from the stars departed, leaving behind the remains of their culture for men to marvel at through the long corridors of time.

Ron Ormond and Ormond McGill at Angkor Wat.

The art and architecture of the vanished Khmers are amazing.
They stand as one of the seven wonders of the world.

Ron Ormond examining one of the strange god-like statues that dot the jungle landscape of this remote area of the world.

*Ron Ormond and Lowell Thomas meet at Angkor Thom
(Reprinted with permission from Ormond McGill's* The Secret
World of Witchcraft, *pub. A. S. Barnes and Company, Inc. 1973).*

IN THAILAND

12

Lahu Religio-Medicine
in the Mountains of Thailand

Medicine (healing) and religion, especially among primitive people, are closely allied. Thus, I very much wanted to get Harold Young's account of how the Lahu medicine men cure their sick with the use of herbs. In Thailand, the Thai dislike the Lahu, and the Lahu return the sentiment. Accordingly, these mountain people remain pretty much to themselves and little is known about them.

Harold M. Young is an American, proprietor of the zoo in Chiengmai; he is one of the few persons in the world who have actually lived among the Lahu. Mr. Young gave me these strange and inside facts about the Lahu medicine men and their methods, of which this is a firsthand report.

The Lahu are a race of aboriginal people who originated in the remote mountains of Burma, from which they have gradually migrated down into northern Thailand. The tribesmen are expert hunters with their crossbows, and seek little communion with people of other races, preferring to live their own lives, in their own way, deep in the mountain wilderness. They are worshippers of spirits (good and evil) and practitioners of an Asian form of voodoo; hence it is little wonder that they are not popular with the native Burmese and Thais, who regard them, and the region they inhabit, with a superstitious tabu. These are the people I chose to investigate.

As I have mentioned, to primitive man, magic, medicine, and religion are almost synonymous terms, the medicine man of a tribe being at once a magician, doctor, and priest. Living their lives always close to nature, such natives possess a rare insight into the

155

Lahu village in the mountains of northern Thailand.

ways of herbal and natural remedies, many of which are undoubtedly worthy of investigation by pharmaceutical scientists.

There is nothing radical about looking to the natural remedies
of primitive people for revolutionary discoveries in the field of modern medicine. For example, Digitalis is made from Mexico's wild
fox-glove, long a natural medicine used in that country. Quinine,
made from the bark of the Cincona tree of Peru, is another, and
the Carcae poison of the Amazon Indians is proving to have won-
derfully beneficial results as a blood-clotting aid to surgery. And, of
course, there are many others of great value to civilized man. But,
as yet, the wonderfully-stocked storehouse of Mother Nature's Pharmaceutical is hardly touched. This journey into the Far East un-
earthed some exciting prospects.

My interest as a naturalist had led me to a correspondence
friendship with Harold Young. Indeed, this friendship was one of
the motivations that led to our journey. As had been planned, Ron
Ormond and I had parted ways temporarily so that he could film
further in Angkor. Through personal meetings with Harold Young,
I was able to pursue this study of a subject I was eager to learn
more about—native medicines.

When I arrived at the Young residence, beautifully situated at
the very base of heavily jungled hills, Mr. Young was already pre-
occupied with one of the local native women who had a severe case
of hives or Urticaria. They came out in huge welts all over her
body, and she was in agony from the intense itching. Despite the

"first aid" which Young administered to her, the hives continued unabated.

After this failure, the woman's husband took off for the nearest Lahu village with a message from Harold Young that was to be spoken to the medicine man of the tribe. Two days later he returned and took the situation immediately in hand as he brought forth from his bag a handful of dangling roots. These he stewed in a pot, making a concentrated brew which he dabbed on the mass of hives covering his wife's body. In less than an hour the inflammation began to fade, and by nightfall the welts were gone.

Startled, I looked at Harold for an explanation. I had counted on the fact that he was rather used to this type of phenomenon, having dealt with natives for years as an official administrator to the tribes of Burma. The naturalist shrugged, then, because of my insistence, asked the man what the roots were that had resulted in this spectacular curing of his wife's hives. I waited expectantly as he put the question in native dialect. A moment later he stated they were merely the roots of a common sting nettle, a weed that can be found growing in abundance in the mountains along the borderline of Thailand and Burma.

The Lahu medicine men use many such types of natural herbal remedies in their pharmaceutical kits. Another one that came early to my attention is for the treatment of shingles or Herpes Zoster. Many western doctors treat the disease in connection with nervous disorders, but the Lahu medicine men go right after the cluster of vesicles, and not only dry them up promptly, but allay the pain at the same time with applications of the milky sap of a small jungle tuber.

Harold told me of a personal experience. He had developed a severe case of shingles while hunting in the Burmese jungles, and did everything he could think of in the emergency to try and ease the intense pains. After nine days and nights of it, he was feeling decidedly low when an old Lahu tribesman approached and asked what was wrong. Young showed him the condition, and the Lahu replied at once, "That is what we call 'Meh Meh.' If it is your wish, I will get something immediately that will ease the pain and dry it up." Assured that nothing could be wished for more, the old man left, and in the matter of an hour brought back some tubers of a vine, known locally by the name of "Na Ye Ka." He pressed out a heavy juice from these, and applied it directly to the shingle sores. Relief was immediate, and that night, Young told me, he enjoyed his first good sleep in over a week. After two more applications the following day, the line of vesicles dried up and have never bothered him since.

Later, on returning to the city of Rangoon, Harold Young mentioned the cure to his English doctor. The physician promptly informed him that he couldn't have actually had shingles, because such a cure was quite impossible.

"Well," Young commented dryly, "I'm not an arguing man, so I let the matter drop. But I know I had the shingles and had it bad, and I know that the juice of those tubers cured it and cured it fast. And to myself I thought, 'Okay Doc, but you're missing an opportunity, for someday I'm going to tell that story to a man wise enough to follow it up and he's going to make a name for himself in medical circles.'"

In the wilds of Thailand and Burma one hardly ever sees or hears of a person suffering with bronchial asthma. As any physician will be only too ready to admit, asthmatic conditions are most difficult to relieve, let alone cure. The Lahu medicine men have nature's remedy for it. They make a strong broth from the blending together of wild globe amaranth and a plant known in their mountain lands as the owl thistle. This concoction is taken regularly for a period of two weeks and is claimed to cure even the worse case.

I wanted a specific case, and asked Harold for one. We were seated about a campfire in the center of a rustic village, late in the evening, when Young told me this story:

"When I was a boy, we lived in a valley where this asthma remedy could not be obtained, and had an Indian cook, named Anthony, who suffered terribly from asthmatic attacks. I can remember my mother propping him up in the cookhouse during one of his spells, and doing what she could to relieve him. At the age of fifty-six he heard of and tried out this remedy of the Lahus and was cured. Anthony was still my cook after he was seventy, and to the day of his death, he never had another attack of asthma!"

This peek behind the door of Mother Nature's Pharmaceutical, as practiced by these remarkable "mountain people," was getting fascinating. I stirred up the campfire and asked for more. Young was most accommodating.

"The treatment for boils and abscesses, as practiced by the Lahus, is interesting. The first thing used is sort of a poultice made from the leaves of the 'A Ku' vine. The young leaves are wilted over hot coals, then put into a mortar and pounded into a pulp. This makes an excellent poultice for bringing the abscess to a head.

"When this drawing has taken place, the medicine man has his own method of lancing. He takes a small iron about the size of a knitting needle which has a bulge on it which controls the depth of the penetration when used. This is fitted through a board so the point protrudes about a quarter of an inch. The iron is then heated in the fire until it is red hot. The piece of wood is placed so the hole comes over the head of the abscess, and the needle is given a quick thrust and withdrawn almost instantly. The abscess is open, and all is done so quickly that the patient hardly has time to know what has happened."

I asked for still more of this unique factual material. Young continued, "There is a small bean that is sometimes used by the Lahus. It is roasted and made into a drink which is both tasty and acts as a mild sedative at the same time. In preparing, the bean is first roasted, then pounded into a powder. In this form it is brewed and made into a drink which is administered to the patient twice a day after meals. It has some very important uses. Old people who have had a stroke resulting in paralysis, and who cannot articulate, are known to be walking and talking after a few weeks' treatment. The improvement lasts until another stroke occurs. Among younger persons, the cure appears permanent.

"Another herb is used by the Lahus to bring back a mother's milk when it dries up too soon. This isn't so important in the States nowadays with modern methods, but here in the mountains it is very important to people to whom only breast-feeding is known. The herb used is a tuber. It is cut up and cooked with the food, and in a few days acts so strongly on the milk glands that lactation becomes profuse.

"One time our dispensary compounder's wife, who had lost her own baby six months previous, wanted to adopt a baby. The mother of the child had been terribly burned in an accident and could no longer nurse the infant, so the parents offered it for adoption. The compounder's wife took the milk-restoring treatment of the Lahus. In a week she was lactating like a new mother. She adopted the baby and nursed it as if it were her own.

"Would you like to hear of the use of animal matter as medicine among the Lahus and other Burmese tribes that prescribe by the methods of the jungle?"

I nodded.

"Among the tribes of the back-country of Burma, for example, the leg bones of leopards and tigers are highly prized. Sambar deer horns in velvet, rhinoceros matter, and the musk of the musk deer are all used for medicinal purposes. The Lahu use only galls, marrow, and fats on a large scale. Bear gall is used widely for sprains and rheumatism. The gall is dried; a little of the dried crystal is dissolved in water and is rubbed directly on the affected part. It is very penetrating and seems to help such conditions with amazing rapidity. I could tell you of many other of these natural remedies, but perhaps it would be more interesting to give a personal experience with the treatment.

"I had a bad knee, some years back, that bothered me for months. I went to one of the government doctors, and he said I would need an operation. It was hunting season, so I decided to go back to the wilds, knee or no knee. When I reached the village, the Lahu medicine man insisted that I give bear gall a try. I did, and within a week my knee was so well I could climb without pain. I continued on with the treatment for a short time, and have never been bothered with it since."

I knew that I was getting valuable information, so I pressed Harold for more.

"Python gall is also highly prized," he went on, after he had refilled and lighted his pipe. "It is used for sore and inflamed eyes. The first time I learned of this gall was when one of the boys in my father's school had a bad eye that would not respond to treatment at the clinic. One old man asked permission to use python gall and assured us it would help a lot. We let him try, and within a week that boy's eye condition was completely cleared up. I was so impressed that I never forgot the incident, and years later when one of our dogs, a very valuable one and much loved, began developing a white film over the pupils of its eyes that cost it its sight, I treated the infected eyes with python gall, and, remarkably, the trouble disappeared. These little crystals of python gall dissolved in water make a greenish liquid that is the most soothing eyewash I have ever known.

"Various kinds of fats are also used by the Lahu for medicinal purposes," Young continued. "Python fat is rendered and is used for the treatment of eczema. This seems to possess special qualities for softening the dry scales. After this has been accomplished, the infection is killed by applying a poultice made from the young leaves of a dwarf variety of locust.

"Tiger fat is said to be one of the most penetrating bases that may be used for making an ointment in which bear, python, or bison gall has been mixed. This salve is effectively used for treating neuralgia, arthritis, and rheumatism. The most prized of all fats is that of the giant bamboo gopher. The rendered fat is applied to sprains and sore muscles, and the unrendered pieces are used to draw out thorns which have been deeply embedded in the flesh. Bear fat is not used for humans, but it is one of the main remedies in treating wounds and cuts on livestock.

"Other interesting remedies are made with crow gall, bison gall, wild goat (Serow) marrow, and various herbs. The crow gall is supposed to promote the growth of hair, and is used by the Lahu to develop a mustache. The bison gall is not regarded as a medicine alone to cure disease, but when taken internally is used as a drug to keep the patient awake. In times of emergency, the Lahu men take this gall and claim that one dose is sufficient to keep them awake for several days. However, the main use of bison gall is as a liniment. And the greasy marrow of the Serow is said to be the best thing to rub on stiffness. It is very penetrating and limbers up the muscles, and when combined with the fat of the bamboo gopher, the two together will relieve pain at the same time."

"Harold," I asked, "before we end this, will you kindly give me a few more herb remedies used by the Lahu medicine men."

Young thought a moment.

"I remember one case of a man's life being saved by the quick application of a melon seed poultice; it happened to my own driver. The man, while cutting through a thicket of bamboo, was bitten by what we call in these parts a 'chasing cobra.' It is an extremely vicious and venomous snake. Fortunately, I knew of this Lahu remedy and luck was with us. The particular striped melon necessary grew in patches close by, so I quickly knifed the wound and applied the seeds. The man is still my driver."

I looked at the naturalist, begging him to continue; he did.

"The medicine made by the seeds of this striped melon is really wonderful. The Lahu medicine men pound them into a pulp and make a poultice for use against all kinds of poisonous stings and snake bites. If the melon seeds are fresh, it seems that the seed-poultice can be made and used directly. But if the seeds are dry, then a little water is added and the wet seeds are mashed and then applied.

"These nature remedies, as used by the Lahu medicine men, have always struck me as remarkable. My driver, who, I just mentioned, we saved from the snake bite by the melon seeds, gave me another striking example you might find interesting.

"One day we ran into a group of native girls, one of whom was especially attractive. My driver was taken with her at once, and later made inquiry as to whether she was married or not. The men of the town emphatically explained that she was not, as no man could go near her, she had such a bad case of 'b.o.'

" 'I will cure her,' my man exclaimed! Later he met the girl and proposed, and married her. Shortly, I asked him how his 'fragrant wife' was.

" 'She is fragrant in a different way now,' he explained, 'for I have cured her the Lahu way.'

"I knew what that meant; the Lahus use a type of mint-like watercress to cure sickness of body glands that secrete obnoxious odors. Although I have not had personal experience with the treatment, it must have worked, for I have seldom seen a more happy couple than my driver and his wife.

"Here's a last one you might like to add to your report. The Lahu have a sobering concoction for drunkeness that is a whiz.

"For this, the natives take the bark of what they call the 'Leum-

La-Hkam' tree, steep it in boiling water, and make a brew. This is drunk by the inebriated man, and he becomes a sober fellow literally in a matter of minutes. It's wonderful. I have often thought, if the proper person, with organic chemical knowledge, would analyze this cure and isolate the basic constituents so it could be made into an easily taken pill of some sort, this Lahu secret alone could be made into a million-dollar industry in the States."

As Harold stopped talking, I found myself thinking deeply about these interesting Lahu medicines and remedies. After a few moments of silence, I asked him point blank, "Harold, would you be willing to have a doctor, medical researcher, or organic chemist come and test your claims and investigate these age-old remedies of the Lahu? If what you describe is true, there may well be new and beneficial drugs of many important kinds that can be isolated from these nature remedies that will be of inestimable value to the growing pharmacy of modern medicine."

Young looked me squarely in the eyes, and answered immediately.

"In India, for centuries, they used an herb that produced peculiar mental effects on those who took it. After years of complete ig-

Ormond McGill and Lahu tribesman.

Ron Ormond and Ormond McGill visit with Siva Namasondhi and his wife in front of the famous "Sleeping Buddha" of Siam. Siva Namasondhi is the official astrologer of the court of Thailand and editor of "Thai Prediction" magazine.

norance on the part of science, enough curiosity was finally generated to start a little investigation that resulted in the discovery of the new drug, Reserpine. This, as you most likely know, is now made from India's Rauwolfia plant and has become a very important auto-hypertensive drug, which has proved of tremendous worth in the treatment of certain types of mental illnesses.

"To answer your question, not only would I be willing to have medical research investigate these cures of the Lahu medicine men, I would be at their service to help them find every needed ingredient for conducting their experiments. As you know, I, with my family, live here in Thailand at Veluvan Villa, Chiengmai. We own and operate the zoo, and so are most definitely permanent residents. I would welcome any technical callers."

When Ron joined me, I told him of this offer; we both wonder who will be the first to take advantage of this unusual opportunity.

Harold Young kindly drove us to the airport and saw us rise

into the sky. Our flight from Thailand took us on to Burma to land in the very old city of Rangoon. I have mentioned in this book how very important Buddhism is to the people of the Orient. Here in this ancient and exotic city is located the central headquarters of all Buddhists throughout the world.

Thus, from Burma, I bring you the message that follows in the next chapter.

Giant "Deamon" guardian at the Temple of Dawn, Bangkok, Thailand.

IN BURMA

13

A Message from the World Headquarters of Buddhism in Burma

Only seven miles from the exotic city of Rangoon is located the Maha Pasana Guha, the "Great Cave of the Buddhists." This is the international headquarters of Buddhism, and nothing like it can be found anywhere else in the entire world.

The Maha Pasana Guha is an artificially-built cave that is a dream come true. Burma's former pious Prime Minister, U Nu, sat in meditation under the Bodhi Tree in Buddha Gaya, India, after having visited the Satta Pani Cave at Rajgir, in the course of a pilgrimage to the Buddhist shrines in that land of magic that cradled the Buddha. It was then that U Nu had a vision of a similar cave in Burma, filled with learned Buddhist monks or Bhikkhus and others from many lands, gathered to spread the Buddha's message of peace and enlightenment for a war-torn and trouble-ridden world. That vision is today a reality.

The Cave was specifically built to hold the Sixth Great Buddhist Synod (the Chatta Cangayana), an international Buddhist study group, which opened on May 17, 1954 and was in continuous session for two years thereafter. In the course of the last 2,498 years, five such councils have been held at intervals of hundreds of years, and each time the inspiration has been to purify, edit, and codify the Buddhist Sacred Texts. From this center of religious learning is developing the International Institute for Advanced Buddhistic Studies with principles surprisingly parallel to those we designed for our own AOPSA, which I wrote about in Chapter Two of this book. It is a center for scholars, eastern or western, specializing in Buddhism and eastern philosophy and culture to strengthen friendship and understanding in the world.

In Burma, there are four kinds of pagodas: 1. Dhatu Zedi, enshrining relics. 2. Pari-bhoga Zedi, enshrining implements or garments of the Buddha or Buddhist saints. 3. Uddissaka Zedi, enshrining the images of the Buddha. 4. Dhamma Zedi, enshrining sacred books.

The famous Shwedagon falls under both the first and second categories and is the largest Buddhist shrine on earth; it is held in the greatest veneration by Buddhists the world over. The Shwedagon was built in 585 B.C., being originally a mere twenty-seven feet in height, and was brought up to its present physical glory and height of 326 feet in the fifteenth century by Shin Sawbu, Queen of Pegu.

For 2500 years the shrine has been regarded as sanctified ground, and the authenticity of its origin is supported in Buddhist scriptures. It is held that a couple of Burmese traders, who had gone over to India, met the Buddha and received a gift of eight hairs from his own head. On their return, this sacred gift was placed by the Burmese king in the pagoda along with sacred relics of three preceding Buddhas (reincarnations) consisting of a staff, a water-dipper, and a bathing garment. All of these revered artifacts were enshrined, giving the Shwedagon a four-fold religious significance and importance to all Buddhists.

Whatever one's personal religious convictions or beliefs, the Buddha story holds a message for all. While in Burma, we were asked to carry that message from the world headquarters of Buddhism; an obligation we are happy to fill, viz.:

The Buddha as a young man was very concerned about the amount of suffering he saw around him, suffering connected with birth, disease, old age, death, running the whole span of man's life.

Eventually he left his father's court, his wife and new-born child to try to discover for men a way of release from suffering. He studied the philosophies of the leading teachers of his day. He underwent every form of asceticism, but in none of these did he find the answer he was seeking.

At last, understanding came to him under the Bo Tree at Buddhagaya. He saw that suffering springs from desire, craving, and lust. To escape from suffering men must get free from material desire and break all bonds of attachment, and the way to do this was to follow the noble eight-fold path of right belief, right aim, right

The famous Shwedagon, Rangoon, Burma.

speech, right action, right livelihood, right effort, right mindfulness, and right contemplation.

This enlightenment gave Buddha the spiritual freedom which he sought for all men. In that moment he could have entered the spiritual state of Nirvana (perpetual bliss for the spirit), but for the sake of all living creatures he decided to stay on in the world and preach his gospel of how to attain perfect peace.

For forty years he wandered, preaching his message in Central India and inspiring a band of devoted disciples who were to carry his teaching in successive generations to every country of the Orient.

At the age of eighty he died and went to that blessed state of Nirvana, the full enjoyment of which he had in the interests of mankind denied himself for so many years. Cessation of selfish desire and emancipation from the three cardinal evils of lust, ill-will, and ignorance must be achieved to obtain Nirvana, spake the Buddha.

Thus ended the message we were asked to carry.

Buddhism emphasizes that every person is the master of his own destiny, his present is the result of his past thoughts and deeds, and his future will be the combined result of his past and present thoughts and deeds. No other individual can help or mar his des-

Maha Pasana Guha (The Great Buddhist Cave).

tiny, but others who by their own efforts have found the true path can show him the way.

Buddha, who founded the religion by his own efforts, has shown the way for others to follow. One of the most honored epithets of Buddha is, therefore, the simple one of "teacher." It is in honor of him that the original Shwedagon was erected, and it is to honor his memory and to be reminded of his teachings that pious Buddhist pilgrims visit the gigantic shrine and the thousands of other wats, temples, and shrines that dot the landscapes of the countries of the East.

Interior of the cave—Sixth Buddhist Synod in session.

14

The Art of Meditation

Buddhism and the art of meditation have a very close alliance, and this latter practice is very important to the people of the Orient. It is especially suited to their way of life, and is directly incorporated into their religions, being sincerely performed (even among the very young), in a variety of forms, in all the lands of the East. Until recently meditation had little meaning to most people in the Occident, but with the trend toward rebellion against the "hurry, hurry, hurry" of western existence, many have turned to it for the finding of relaxation and inner peace, and young intellectuals have found in it a method of expanding consciousness and self-awareness. A wave of popularity for meditation has been sweeping the western nations.

The people of the Orient have a very worthwhile contribution to give to the people of the Occident in the practice of meditation. Not only is it psychologically beneficial, it likewise disciplines the mind and turns it toward reverence as it goes within to seek the God Source.

The art of meditation is a skill in the directing of thought in procedures of concentration. Through it the student learns how to control the mind. As Guru Nanak, the great master and founder of Sikhism in India said, "Conquer the mind and you conquer the world."

Further, meditation arouses latent powers within; powers possessed by everyone, but laying dormant in most people. Before we consider the actual technique of meditation, some understanding of the meaning of Samadhi or Vipassana will be helpful. "Going within," what does it mean? It means simply going beyond the limiting

172

Close neighbors: the Kaba Aye (Pagoda of World Peace) and the Maha Pasana Guha (the Great Buddhist Cave), Burma.

experience of our five senses, and entering the region of inner-reality. In advanced meditation, the physical body is made senseless, the mind is stilled, and the spirit of the individual is raised to a state of superconsciousness. Doors of hidden truth and mysteries of the universe are opened. To the master of meditation, the whole world becomes crystal clear, sources of knowledge are his, and the secrets of the soul are laid bare as the "Kingdom of Heaven" is found within.

Jesus the Christ spoke thus of this "Kingdom of Heaven" within:

"What? Know ye not that your body is the temple of the Holy Ghost, which is in you?" 1 Cor. 6:19.

In the Aquarian Gospel, Jesus talks about meditation to a Magus who asked, "From whence does your wisdom come and what is the light?" To which Jesus answered, "There is a silence where the soul may meet its God, and there a fount of wisdom is, and all who enter are immersed in light, filled with wisdom, love and power."

While on our journey, Ron Ormond and I studied meditation at the feet of Guruni Varamei, Thailand's great woman master of Vipassana (the Siamese method of meditation); in India under Sadhu Satish Kumar, who instructed us in the unique Hindu beliefs and methods; and under Guruni Siu Ho Yang, in Taiwan, who gave us a method of meditation that is especially useful to occidental students.

It was Guruni Varamei who first introduced us to the subject. Her basic philosophy of the study was wonderful. She stated: "The average mind is like the oceans during a storm when the waters are violently agitated. Each gust of wind is a storm of passion, of desire, of duty that must be accomplished, of a hundred-and-one other irritations, anxieties and detours of the mind. Proper concentration (meditation) is the cure."

I will present some further insights into this subject from different eastern countries.

The Yogi of India often speak of the Kundalini, or sleeping serpent power. Their method of meditation is designed to awaken the Kundalini. It is accomplished, they say, through arousing the seven psychic centers, known as "the seven lotuses" (or Chakras). This is manifested through what is called the two currents of Prana, which flow along the channel of the spinal cord, called the Sushuma. According to India's adepts, Prana is the sum-total of all force in the universe, mental and physical. The two currents of Prana in the body are the positive current, called Pingala, and the negative current, called Ida. The spinal cord is held to have an invisible channel in its center known as the Sushuma, through which pass these positive and negative currents. The correct processes of breathing are said to set these currents in motion within the Sushuma, culminating in the influencing of psychic faculties in the brain.

Thus, during meditation, with the aid of proper methods of breathing, the seven Chakras can be aroused and energized by ascending the Kundalini (the energizing of the seventh at the base of the brain being termed "the flowering of the lotus"), thereby setting into motion and activity various phases and forms of psychic powers within the individual. Also, the Kundalini is regarded as being closely allied with the creative energies, the sex energies, longevity, etc. As the adepts describe it, "The Kundalini is the entrance to the fountain of youth."

Some of the Hindus like arousing the Kundalini through the practice of a *kirtan* (religious song-fest), and in this they are not alone, as the performance of *mantrans* for meditation is observed throughout the Orient.

Using the *mantran* to achieve meditation is frequently referred to as "the mechanical means." In other words, a method of mechanically activating the vibration of the initiate. Instead of using the powers of will for this purpose, practitioners are helped along with a succession of sounds, repeated over and over.

In subsequent chapters of this book, further mention of these processes will be described in connection with our adventures in India.

In India, Burma, Thailand, Vietnam, Taiwan and other sections of the Orient, each race has formulated its own method of meditation—"of going within," or as some refer to it, "entering the silence."

Here are some mantrans used in different countries for entering meditation.

In Thailand, "Om, Mani, Padme, Hum," meaning to the Thai,

"O Jewel of the Lotus, Amen," is chanted repeatedly in their Buddhist Wats. However, it should be pointed out that while the *mantran* is verbal and done in a rather sing-song manner, there are those among the Buddhists (notably, Wat Pak Nam in Bangkok) that prefer to enter the "silence" silently, *mentally* chanting the mantran rather than vocalizing it.

In India, Pakistan and other areas where the religion of Mohammedanism is practiced, the Moslems chant, "La Allah, Illah Allah," which, translated, means, "Allah is the only God."

Chanting is also an integral part of orthodox Judaism.

Roman Catholics, likewise, make use of the *mantran* principle (under a different terminology, of course) in their chanting over and over, "Hail Mary," and the priests' chant of "Gloria Tibi Dominie" or "Et Com Spiritu Tuo."

The vibrations of the repetitive sounds seem to affect the receptiveness of the mind to spiritual influences.

According to the sages of India, the basis of all sounds is OM (AUM). The first letter, "A," pronounced "Ah" is the root of the sound, pronounced without touching any part of the tongue or palate. They will also tell you that Aum or Om signifies the principles of creation.

Mantran rhythms are equally important to the faiths of the Chinese, namely, Buddhism, Taoism, and Confucianism.

Mantrans are useful to some people, while others find them disturbing. In Thailand, as I have commented, there is a method of meditation called Vipassana which discards verbal sounds and emphasizes a silent method. I will give a little insight into this procedure, viz.:

Select someplace, as free as possible from noises and other disturbances. Darken the room to what appears to be the half-way point between darkness and light; now withdraw yourself from the outside world, and, as Guruni Varamai in Thailand taught us, enter into the closet and shut the door. By "closet" I mean your inner self, the spiritual you. Next say the words to this effect, "Thou abidest within me—Thou art alive there now; Thou hast the power, the glory; Thou are the answer to all that I could ever desire." Now, commence a few rhythmical breathing exercises, drawing the breath in through the nose deeply and slowly. Know, above all, that you are psychically breathing at the same time you are physically breathing, hence arousing the latent powers of the Kundalini at the base of the spine. Next attempt to cause it to slowly mount up the Sushuma channel in the spinal cord. The ascending course should begin to arouse and energize the seven Chakras and set into activity the various phases of psychic and spiritual powers within you.

If you find your mind wandering, bring it back, saying, "It is

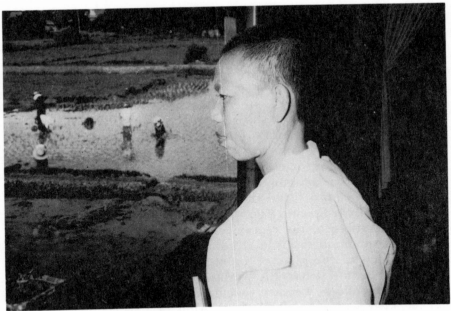

Guruni Varamai at Wat Pak Nam in Bangkok, Thailand.

being done, all that I want to accomplish is being done, and I am receiving the power to accomplish my end results."

"Be quiet and know" is not a command; it is a way to truth. Knowledge from within cannot come to us unless we are quiet. Even though the world about is seething with turmoil, inwardly, we must know and feel that all is quiet and we are at peace.

If we wish to open the way and allow "it" to come, we must do so with stillness; a stillness combined with trust, patience, and receptive listening.

Let us explore this receptive listening. Guruni Varamai expresses it beautifully: "Enter the silence and harken to the Voice of the Soul. It is within the mind-self (soul) that we find the storehouse of wisdom; to listen then is to learn the conscious entrance into that storehouse."

Why now is this "storehouse" thus filled with knowledge? There are two answers. From the West, we have a reservoir of accumulated knowledge gleaned of experience and memories, stored in the subconscious, with infinite associations to draw upon. And from the East, it is held that within us we have the truths gleaned of repeated incarnations and of the soul's vibrative energy reaching to the "Source," which agrees with the words of the adept, "The soul of the child is as mature as the soul of the sage."

Guruni Varamai, Thailand's remarkable woman exponent of "Vipassana," with Ron Ormond and nun-initiates in her shrine. Students begin the study of meditation at an early age and become masters of the art.

Oriental wisdom appreciates that the soul has been gathering value to itself for many ages, and that if we discover how to consciously enter that sacred realm, its treasure will be our conscious possession. And to each is given the right and power to enter into this temple of infinite supply and help himself (or herself) to all his fondest desires.

How does one enter the state of meditation and help one's self to this temple of infinite supply? Such was our cry in the Orient, and the masters told us, "Patience students, and understand. To wish to enter the silence is a mark of a master, but on entering it one of the first things you will learn is that the solving of one's personal problems and benefiting of self is a wasted life; learning to live that all men may benefit is the true goal."

For "entering the silence" and "going within" are not ways of entering an introverted life of self-satisfaction, but rather are marks of your higher evolvement that will bring you in closer oneness with your fellow humans and the God Source.

I do not mean to imply that meditation cannot help one in the solution of problems, but to enter meditation for such shallow purposes is entirely the wrong approach and narrows your sphere of development. Keep your purpose big and large in altruism, and your personal concerns will be entirely solved as "by-products," as you reach through to greater things.

This verse correctly conveys the thought:

> Think not that to gain your wish
> You must so and so believe,
> Forget not the truth of this,
> Meditate first, then, ask,
> And you receive.

In other words, meditate because you want to become one with God. If you do this, then all things will come unto you.

As I mentioned previously, Ron and I studied meditation in Thailand, India, and Taiwan. The art of meditation is inherent in many oriental religions, however it is by no means an exclusive property of the Orient. Many western students have today mastered the practice. The method we have found most useful in teaching others was that taught us by Guruni Siu Ho Yang, Buddhist instructress of meditation in Taipei. Her method can be grasped readily and put to use by occidental people. This is her instruction:

First, it is important that you learn to sit and be still physically. Select an hour in the day or evening where and when you can be absolutely free from interruptions. It is important that you select an especial hour, one that you can take each day, and use no other.

This is to become your *special hour;* your hour of meditation. In time, you will come to look forward to it eagerly and with anticipation; for within that hour will come to you a sense of ecstasy, a feeling of belonging; within that hour you will come to recognize your divine heritage and the awakening of your higher consciousness.

Now, during your selected hour and within your room of quiet privacy, sit upright in a chair. Place both feet flat on the floor; a right angle should be formed at the knee. Do not slump in the chair, but sit erect; keeping the spinal column straight.

Such is your physical position for meditation. Next you must turn your attention to your thoughts. When you first practice the art

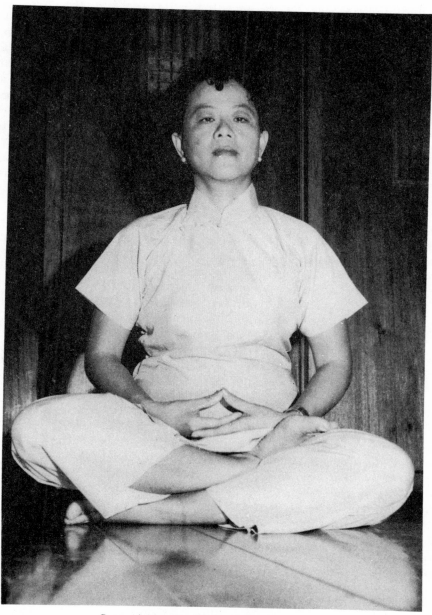

Guruni Siu Ho Yang, Taipei, Taiwan.

you will unquestionably experience difficulty in controlling them for the first week or so. So don't try; just let them run wherever they will, and know that in due time they will quiet and submerge into the proper discipline.

Remember, your first and only discipline during the learning process is physical—"Be quiet and know." In a short time, as you advance, your thoughts will be automatically controlled. And with your acquired discipline will come a time when you will be able to stop during a stroll and find a delightful stillness surrounding you, and your mind will be absolutely free.

So let me repeat, master first physical control. Sit still and be quiet. Breathe evenly and regularly. Master all nervous movements. Just sit upright in quiet and stillness; your eyes but slightly open looking at nothing in particular, thinking nothing in particular, just waiting in stillness.

It sounds easy, but it is not; not at first. Later it will become a pleasure.

After a week or so of practice of physical control of the stillness of the body, a stillness of the mind will come. Once this has arrived, commence to command your thoughts. Send your thoughts on simple errands first, viz., send them within your body to different parts such as your right hand, your left hand, your feet, your stomach, etc. Try to trace every sensation you feel as you direct your thoughts to the different areas. And, with your thoughts, an increased supply of blood will go to the different areas that you will sense as a tingling or a warmth. Practice this exercise of the direction of thought and the study of these sensations for a few sessions.

You are now ready for your next advancement, the study of images.

To visualize requires intellect; in its exercise it calls on both memory and imagination. Let your first imaging be of the real; not of the ideal. Let it be of, say, a city you visited long ago. Call up in memory all it was. And, passively waiting, enjoy, as you can, looking at these mental pictures. Do this practice in visualization for a few days, and soon you will find the mental pictures becoming more and more distinct. Some details you had not even noticed when you first visualized will now appear. A street you scarcely recognized comes to your vision. A week or two of these sittings and your powers of visualization will greatly expand.

Through your practice in learning the art of meditation, thus far, you have learned to master your body so you can sit erect and in stillness; you have learned to follow implanted thought sensations in your body; you have quieted your mind and have trained it in the practice of visualization.

You have learned a great deal, and this initial training is an im-

portant part of your developing skill. For, through this practice, you
will have begun to open a source of communication into your "inner-
self"—the seat of the soul.

By no means have you as yet advanced to that stage of development where you can sit down like an adept and meditate, but you
are on your way, and through your practice are being taught to
"wire in" to that inner creative force through which lies the path
to expanded consciousness, self-awareness, and knowledge.

You are now at the stage in your training when you must seriously
begin to contemplate the purpose of your meditation. As has been
previously mentioned, set your scope big, your ideals high, your horizons magnificent. Let there be not one selfish motive behind your
desire to learn this great art of "going within," and it will truly
bring you the "Kingdom of Heaven" while still living in the human
body, as the oriental masters express it.

Everyone receives some stimulus from nature's sublime forces, but
only to a limited extent. The adept can become the focal center of
such stimulus; meditation greatly increases one's sensitivity in this regard. There will occur times in your meditative practice when it
will seem that you are receiving thoughts and commands from the
outside. This can be good or it can be harmful. The thought, the
commands that come must be judged and tried. If the thoughts are
good and from a high spiritual source they can be of great value.
But if they are low and base, beware and turn them down. Remember, you can stand alone in the eyes of God and constantly
receive help from within yourself, as you are now beginning to
learn how to tap the inner power that can do all things. This is why
it is so strongly stressed that you set your purpose always high, that
the power you develop may bring about good.

As you advance in your skill at meditation, you will notice also
that you begin to go out beyond the individual or conscious self,
and will find that you reach out mentally to others.

I have advised you to beware and judge the incoming thoughts
that you will sense, yet here I have mentioned a deliberate reaching
out for such thoughts. There is no contradiction meant. You must
reach, as your inner-self released will instinctively seek oneness with
all humanity. This truth is summed up in the following statement
from the oriental masters: "Thou art that." It means that *this* individual is *that* individual. In other words, that each individual has
a oneness with every other individual; all mankind is one spirit, one
essence, and should regard itself as a living part of infinite life.
Truly the doctrine of Universal Oneness.

This again is why your purpose, your goal in meditation must
be set high and be designed for the benefit of all mankind, removed
from all selfish motive. To the student, let me say most sincerely,

unless you aim your meditation thus, toward high ideals, it is an art best left unlearned.

To continue with your instructions for developing skill in meditation.

At your sessions now, select some purpose most unselfish in itself and directly affecting the good of another whom you know. If you are aware that he is asleep when you are meditating, endeavor to help and treat him for his ills or needs.

To do this, place yourself in the silence, and visualize him where he is, and see yourself as near him; then speak your wisdom to his soul. You will be surprised how quickly the work will be done. In your practice, always preserve the attitude of listening—to allow him to unburden himself. Remember, intuition speaks more frequently through the medium of the mental ear than through that of mental sight.

Now, here are some details of modes-of-procedure that will aid you in your advancing practice.

When you first begin your meditative periods do so with your eyes open, but keep them downcast on a position near the knees. As your eyes become strained, close them gently; the feeling will calm you and create a fine mood for your session.

The lights of the room in which you practice should always be subdued. Soon your eyes will become accustomed to the lack of light and everything will stand out as perfectly as need be. Physical sight is of little consequence in the art of meditation; it is the inner sight of the soul that you seek.

As you proceed with your practice, it is well to begin to discipline your method of breathing. Here is a simple exercise in this regard that will be found helpful.

Inhale, counting 1,2,3,4. Hold the breath in your lungs for the same count; then exhale counting the same. Now, rest four more counts. Then do the exercise again and again. Before long, you will not be counting at all, and this rhythm to your breathing will become automatic. This directed process of breathing harmonizes the system and fits you for more advanced work.

Let us now proceed a step further in this control of breath.

Press your forefinger against your right nostril, and inhale deeply through the open left nostril. As you do this, center your thought on the Kundalini (dormant, psychical fluid) within your spinal column. As you reach it mentally, you will feel the "serpent" stir. Now, concentrate on sending your breath through it so that it may strike mentally on the last plexus—the base of the spine—the seat of the Kundalini. Hold the breath you have taken in, thus, through your left nostril; then release the right nostril, compress the left, and exhale through the right. This practice will increase your control and power.

After you have followed these methods and conducted your practice meditative sessions for a matter of months, the realization will begin to dawn upon you that a change is gradually developing, and you will begin to experience periods of complete bliss when you cease to strive for anything and are just content to bask in the inner-sense of glory that you feel. This is the beginning of real meditation; you have established the pathway to the soul.

You can now terminate your "same hour" daily sessions, and keep the path open by fifteen-minute sessions at different times of the day or night, for once the path is open, it is yours to tread when and as you choose.

And, as you enter the silence as a master and plumb the depth of the soul, there is no limit to the wonders it can spread before you, as through it you reach out in oneness to the God-Source and all the universe.

Just a word of caution at this point in your development. Do not strain to reach that which does not appear of itself through these avenues. Be content with whatever your meditation brings you. If you desire knowledge of a sort, seek it, but do not strain for it. "It" is within the storehouse and will come forth when the time is ready and you have advanced to the stage when you can both use and find it.

As you progress further, you will create an atmosphere about yourself that can hold and receive the vibrations that you are calling to yourself, and the revelations from your soul will become more revealing and meaningful as they pass into your consciousness. A new seriousness and purposefulness will begin to dominate your life. You will sense a new understanding of all things, a unity in all, and a sense of time that is simply an eternal "now." In the brilliant radiance of the present and the knowing that it is always yours, you have a constant treasure of inestimable value.

You who would learn meditation, remember that the art is not just an experience; it is a practice that leads literally to spiritual advancement and growth. The unfolding can come no faster than you are ready to absorb. The actual power of the soul and its revelations are without limit; what it can bring you, personally, depends entirely upon your spiritual growth. The limitless powers of the soul are in reality the limitless powers of *man*, for man is soul incarnate. Even though no mortal ("in body man") can ever reach the pinnacles of the sublime heights that are possible, every approach toward it is upliftment to worthier deeds and nobler living. History shines with names that tell of what great things man has done. Ask yourself now, "What have I done?" Ask yourself if you are ready for this absolute unity of all life and its great forces?

If your answer is, "Yes!" then begin to make your path that leads within the soul. Meditate.

Ancient statue of the Buddha performing meditation in the western style.

After you have entered session after session of meditation and proved the truth of this philosophy by receiving revelations from the soul, do not hesitate to assert your oneness with the Creative Force and Universal Powers, and sing with Emerson:

"I am the owner of the spheres,
Of the seven stars and solar years,
Of Caesar's hand and Plato's brain,
Of Lord Christ's heart,
And Shakespeare's strain."

It was in Rangoon that we took the big Viscount that was to land us at Dum-Dum airport in Calcutta for the last lap of our strange journey into the unknown. India lay before us. As we soared over the vast Bay of Bengal, both Ron and I felt a thrill as though somehow we sensed that here in "the land of magic" our adventures would mount to a hair-raising climax.

IN INDIA

15

Buried Alive in India

There is a bit of the daredevil in each of us; Ron Ormond has more than his share. In India, the Hindu fakirs sometimes perform the feat of being buried alive. Having witnessed it, Ron found himself involved in trying it for himself. He tells the story.

Panic rose in my throat, and I wanted to scream, but couldn't, as the last grey shaft of light disappeared above my head and I was in darkness. I sat cross-legged in the small hole, a human skull resting on my lap, seeming to weigh a ton. Dully, I heard another spadeful of dirt crash upon the boards over my head, and particles of it trickled down around me. The sound of the next shovelful was less audible and I lay there in the cramped darkness, listening to the harsh, labored sounds of my own breathing, wondering whether my nerves were going to crawl out the tips of my fingers.

I had volunteered to be buried alive; I most fervently wished I hadn't. The thought that this shallow hole in the ground thousands of miles from home was in reality my potential grave was nerve-wracking. Already the air was becoming stale in my makeshift tomb, and I wondered whether I would be able to hold out the full hour I had agreed to remain.

Panic was welling over me, again, with the force of a tidal wave and flashing thoughts of my wife and son, in far-off California, engulfed me for a moment.

Buried alive in India—what a way to die!

Above me, standing beside the mound of dirt, watching the Indian natives tamp down the surface to insure against any breathing

189

hole and nervously eyeing his watch, would be my partner, Ormond McGill. He had told me I was crazy to try this, but I had insisted. Now there was nothing he could do for me. Not until my hour— or my life—was up.

In India, the feat of the fakirs of being "buried alive" now is prohibited by law; too many deaths have resulted from unsuccessful performances.

But this country, with its unorganized, teeming millions, still has fakirs who will perform the strange rite for a consideration in rupees.

While in Calcutta, we had contacted G. Kumar, an East Indian considered one of India's leading teachers of magicians. Kumar and Ormond McGill had a great deal in common, for my partner had toured the world several times with his show of magic and hypnotism. Indeed, had it not been for the mutual respect Kumar had for McGill in the field of magic, I would never have ended up in a black hole in Calcutta with a ton or so of India's earth over my head.

After a lengthy explanation of what we sought, Kumar had introduced us to a young fakir named Manoram, who assured us he had performed the "buried alive" feat many times. After considerable discussion and a promise of total secrecy lest the law step in, he had agreed to carry out the seemingly impossible stunt for our movie camera.

Through Kumar's interpretation, we learned that Manoram started practicing as a fakir at the age of nine, becoming a professional at fourteen, when he had first undergone the suspended animation act of being buried alive. He now was a handsome young man of twenty-four. If he had been practicing his strange calling for ten years, we reasoned, it was unlikely anything could go wrong.

It was a bright Sunday morning when we kept our secret rendezvous, accompanied by G. Kumar. The word "secret" can be only loosely interpreted. A hole some three feet deep had already been dug in a yard surrounded by a high wall, and a crowd of some forty Indians were there, waiting and expectant.

As we planned to photograph the entire sequence, Mac and I carefully set up our movie equipment, while Manoram disappeared into a shed.

The hole resembled a grave in which the corpse was to be buried in a sitting position, as we had seen practiced among the aborigines in other parts of the Orient. Mac, acquainted with magicians' methods, searched for any hidden air hose or similar breathing supplement. There was nothing. Only the hole.

Manoram reappeared with Kumar. The change in his appearance was startling.

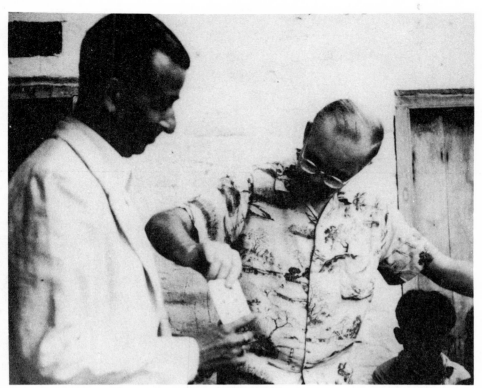

Ormond McGill performs a bit of card-conjuring for Hindu magic instructor, G. Kumar.

Ron Ormond shoots popular fakir feats of snake-charming and magic on the streets of Calcutta.

Ormond McGill, (seated center), with magicians in India. Seated on his right is G. Kumar, India's leading magic instructor. On his left, K. Lal, India's master stage illusionist. (Rear) Ron Ormond standing with magic students of Kumar.

The fakir, Manoram, preparing himself to be "buried alive," with Ron Ormond photographing the proceedings.

Ormond McGill examines the skull held by Manoram, Hindu master of suspended animation.

He had entered the shed a well-dressed young Hindu, and emerged a traditional fakir. Dressed only in a wrapping of native cloth, a string of wooden beads encircling his neck, and his features painted with a gaudy red arrow at the bridge of his nose; he was clutching a human skull!

A hush came over the Hindu gathering and several raised their hands in the prayerful sign of the *namaste* as he approached.

Seating himself by the side of the grave, he crossed his legs with the soles of his feet turned upwards Buddha-fashion. With the skull in his lap, he closed his eyes and a total silence fell on the crowd. Not even the flies which had buzzed persistently about us seemed to move now.

After several minutes, with eyes still closed, his body rigid and legs crossed in this contortionistic pose, the fakir was picked up by the attendants and lowered into the grave.

Mac and I had been filming the entire sequence of events. This was the type of material we sought. A series of boards were placed

Manoram enters the grave to be "buried alive."

over the head of the fakir and shovelful after shovelful of dirt was heaped upon the scant covering until a mound of earth had been built over the entombed Indian.

Guru Kumar then took a heavy metal weight and began methodically tamping down the loose earth, packing it tightly over the grave to insure against any air holes.

As he stepped back, we glanced up at the crowd; it had grown surprisingly, despite the supposed secrecy. Fully one hundred persons now stood silently watching the smooth mound, as though realizing the danger to one of their own kind, who lay buried at their feet.

Manoram had said he would stay buried alive in the narrow confines of the grave for three hours, and we waited for the time to tick off on our watches. About us, the Indians—despite their natural stoicism—were beginning to fidget, some of them casting hostile glances toward Mac and myself.

When a human life is involved, hours multiply themselves. I was becoming apprehensive myself, as the end of the third hour neared and I glanced at Mac, who was staring at the solidly-packed mound of dirt, his expression a study in anxiety.

"Think he'll come out of there okay?" I wanted to know.

He answered without looking at me. "He'd better. This is illegal! Remember?"

Tension was building up among the Hindus as time moved with weighted hands, and there were low murmurings as well as more hard glances in our direction. There was no telling what the Indians might do if the experiment failed. His death would certainly be on our hands, as we were foreigners and the ones who had asked that the feat be performed. Even Kumar, the teacher of magic, was casting uneasy glances toward the waiting crowd.

What had started as a quiet Sunday morning of filmmaking had all the ingredients of an international incident!

At the end of the third hour, Kumar directed the assistants to the grave. The crowd moved forward in a wave and we began to roll the color movie-film through our camera.

Tension covered the gathering with a blanket of silence. The only sounds were the cogs of our camera and the grating of the shovels as the earth was removed.

The boards came into view and were quickly placed aside. There in the grave, still seated upright in his rigid, cross-legged position, was Manoram. His eyes were still closed, his breathing imperceptible. A green-gray pallor was behind the darker pigments of his skin, and he appeared dead!

Dropping to their knees at the edge of the hole, two of his attendants gripped the Indian beneath the shoulders and hauled him up. He was as rigid as if rigor mortis had set in as he was placed carefully upon the ground beside the grave. His eyes still remained closed and there was no sign of breathing even yet. Slowly his legs were unknotted from their cramped, unnatural position, and the fakir was stretched prone on the ground.

Resurrection began.

The assistants, working with hurried skill, massaged his muscles, breathed in his face, pumped his chest, paused, searching for signs of life.

There was nothing. No spark.

The Hindus continued with their reviving labors, while McGill and I looked to Kumar for advice or reassurance. He ignored us, shouting suggestions and instructions to those working over the seemingly dead Indian.

Then—after what seemed a thousand years—the fakir began to breathe, and color returned to his face. He sat up slowly, opening his eyes. He looked about, then rested his gaze upon Mac and myself, smiling briefly.

There was a gutteral cry from one of the Hindus behind us, followed by shouts of agreement.

Manoram struggled to his feet and began to argue with the crowd, shaking his head and spreading his hands. The man who had aroused the excitement of the others kept motioning to me excitedly. Actually, he was encompassing both Mac and myself, but I felt as though he had singled me out.

"What is it? What's wrong?" Mac was asking Kumar.

The East Indian shook his head, trying to hide his own disturbance. "He is a troublemaker."

"But what does he want?"

Kumar was looking at me when he answered in simple words, "He says it does not take much courage to photograph and take notes, but it does to play a game with death. He wants to know why you do not volunteer to be buried alive yourself."

Now, months later, I cannot say what went through my mind at that instant. I remember turning to glance at the tall, gaunt troublemaker, and those behind him, and at Manoram, who was arguing angrily.

Suddenly I found myself saying, "I'll do it."

"You're crazy, Ron," Mac declared. "I admit you are a pretty apt student of meditation, but suspended animation is another thing."

"I can stay in that hole for an hour," I told him. It didn't sound like my own voice that was styling those words. "But get me out of there then!"

Manoram argued with me, but while someone explained to his admirers what I proposed, he finally acquiesced—with reluctance—to let me try it for "a few minutes only."

When the Indians knew what I meant to do, their chidings turned to enthusiasm; under their prodding, Manoram finally agreed I should be buried for an hour.

I glanced at the crowd and saw the expectant expressions on the horde of faces. Maybe they didn't know it, but I was scared. And it was too late to back out!

I moved to the edge of the hole and stepped down into it. Settling myself, I assumed much the same position I had seen the fakir take earlier and looked up expectantly. Mac came to the edge of the hole to look down at me.

"You can still change your mind," he advised.

There was nothing I wanted to do more at that point, but neither Mac nor I had reckoned on Kumar.

"It is too late for mind-changing now," he shook his head, indicating the crowd.

Manoram came forward and squatted at the edge of the hole, handing me the skull. Before I could ask his reason for this, he turned his back and walked away. G. Kumar motioned to the

Ron Ormond looks wistfully up out of the hole in which he is to be "buried alive."

fakir's assistants; faltering, looking to the magic teacher for guidance, they moved forward and began to place the boards over my head.

Darkness closed in and the first shovelful of dirt began to rain upon the boards above me. Already a slight pain was shooting through my legs, twisted as they were into this cramped, impromptu "lotus position," as the Buddhists call it. The skull in my hands was smooth and hard. Idly, I wondered who it might have been.

The burying of Ron Ormond.

Then I was laughing ironically. I was being buried alive beneath a ton or so of dirt, and I was worried about the identity of a skull!

When the laughter died in my throat, I was shaking. I took a deep breath, and the air already smelled stale. How much time could have passed? No more than a few minutes. The sound of dirt being piled on my grave could still be heard, although it now was muffled.

I had noticed an ant in the hole near my foot just before I had been handed the skull. Now it bothered me. I could feel it crawling on me, I was sure. It was completely dark in the hole, but I strained my eyes, trying to see my arm, to see if the ant was there.

Somehow, time ceases to have much meaning in a dark, silent hole, and I realized to my surprise that I hadn't the slightest idea how long I had been buried. When were they going to dig me up, I asked myself? It was so silent within those earthen walls. Why didn't somebody make some noise up topside? Had they gone and left me? And that air was getting fouler!

The idea of lowering my head between my legs entered my mind. Near the dirt floor of the hole the air seemed a bit better, but how long would it remain breathable, I wondered?

We had agreed on one hour for the duration of the experiment. Up above it had seemed a short time, but down here—an indeterminable age!

Thoughts raced through my mind; if only those men above would dig me up. Where was Mac? Again came that breath of stale air, and again I nearly panicked. I wanted to shout, to call out for help, but I realized the heap of earth above me would muffle any sound I made, just as it cut off sounds coming down to me. Also, I didn't dare waste my air in shouting.

I waited on in silence, my heart pounding in my breast like a triphammer. I inched my head lower between my legs to get as close to the fresh air, which, I had been told, stays near the bottom of a sealed room or a hole such as this. Suddenly the skull I had been holding in my lap rolled to the dirt below. Momentarily I felt sorry for it—the remains of what had once been a man—my partner for an hour.

McGill and I, in our travels through the Orient, had always tried diligently to hold an extremely sympathetic attitude toward the beliefs of the people we met. Many of these civilizations of the East are very ancient, and are possessed of secrets and customs based on traditions long lost. This attitude of understanding and lack of skeptical criticism had helped greatly in having many strange and unusual things shown to us; things that the average tourist would never even guess at. Suddenly, in my present plight, I thanked my lucky stars for this esoteric interest, for I recalled the practice of Buddhist "Vipassana" that I had learned in Thailand from Guruni Varamai. This process of meditation struck me as resembling very closely the entranced state that Manoram had placed himself into. If it kept him alive in this confined space for three hours, I reasoned, it should keep me alive for only a third of that period. I resolved to try it!

Erecting my body at right angles to my crossed legs, I centered my attention, as I had been taught, on that psychic center some call "the third eye," that lies buried in the brain tissue in back of the middle of the forehead. Slowly I began going over my body, step by step in my mind's eye, in the process I had learned from Thailand's great woman guru. Gradually, the great calm of meditation began to descend on me. With it came a removal of the fear

I had felt, and the stress for breath that had appalled me, vanished. My senses turned inward; time seemed to melt away.

I felt a rude shaking of my shoulders and slowly awareness flowed from deep within my being to perceive what lay without. My eyes opened, and involuntarily closed tightly shut again from the impact of the bright sunlight. Gradually I returned to normal; my experience of being "buried alive" in India was completed.

Later that afternoon, in our hotel room, Mac plied me with questions. I told him everything I remembered. Afterward I shot a few questions of my own to him, questions I would ordinarily have no way of knowing, were it not for the fact that he remained topside, while I sat buried in the grave.

"How did the crowd react? What apprehension gripped you during the entombment? Did you have the urge to dig me out at any time?" I asked.

Even while I sat buried alive with a ton of dirt heaped over my head, my partner, probably more to remain occupied than anything else, made notes. I smiled at this vignette, knowing his personality as I do. I could well imagine the sullen looks he received during this seemingly casual operation. However, I knew that every word must have been written under duress.

I am including a few of his notes in this account of being "Buried Alive in India," for the reader's edification.

FROM ORMOND McGILL'S NOTEBOOK

It is now 3:35 p.m. and Ron has been buried only five minutes. There is no danger—yet. I wonder how he is taking it down there?

3:55 p.m. Less than a half hour has passed. It seems that the hour period will never get over. The Hindus have settled down. Kumar just stepped over to state that Ron is doing a fine thing for America; it shows American courage. Wonder what Ron would reply to that!

4:10 p.m. There is a feeling of danger in the air. Even the Hindus are beginning to fidget as though they wish they hadn't forced this. Ron and I figured that an hour in that grave, without some special process being resorted to, would find the air in that small hole dangerously poisonous. An hour would have been fatal to the average man, and staying buried for three hours, as Manoram did, would be impossible—that is, unless one were willing to die. "Die"; I must not think of that word.

How did Manoram manage the feat; did he place himself in complete suspended animation, in which the fakir literally almost "dies?" Our studies have shown us many convergent states of meditation where the body functions become greately lowered. Indeed, some fakirs even claim they do die temporarily. Perhaps the fakir indulges in a samadhi condition, or what in our western terms might be called autohypnosis. Such could manifest a slackening of the body functions and greatly lessen the need for air. Whatever the explanation, it goes without saying that we have witnessed a miracle. That the feat of being "buried alive" as practiced by the fakirs is genuine is an obvious fact. It has been repeatedly performed. Equally obvious is the fact that many attempts of its performance are unsuccessful, as testified to by the deaths reported.

4:30 p.m. The hour is up. They're digging the dirt away. Some of the Hindus are applauding. Kumar's face is all smiles. Ron is okay. I can close this notebook now.

As I read my partner's notes a feeling of satisfaction came over me. Now we had a picture from personal experience covering the buried-alive feat from both above and below. By the same token, I must admit I would hesitate to volunteer again without plenty of time to consider the circumstances and the possible outcome.

"Buried alive" is becoming a passing phase of Indian mysticism as the law and order of the new Indian government become more stringent. But as far as Mac and I are concerned, this is entirely alright.

———

While in India, Ron involved himself in another harrowing experience: a vigil in the Sacred Room of Provoo Jagadbandhu, which I will tell of in Chapter Eighteen. But first, I want you to meet Sadhu Parimal Bandhu, who introduced him to the room.

16

The Secret Knowledge
of Sadhu Parimal Bandhu

It has been wisely said that the best study of mankind is man himself. To ask oneself the questions of what we are, whence did we come, and whither are we bound is a sign of the maturing of wisdom. In short, the search for full knowledge of ourselves—physically, mentally, and spiritually—is the mark of growth.

While in India, Ron Ormond and I met a man who contributed much to our growth. The man's name was Sadhu Parimal Bandhu. Sadhu is simply an identification of rank in India, in this case meaning priest or teacher. But Parimal Bandhu was far more than a priest or teacher; he was a true sage. I knew him well, but since Ron knew him better and spent long hours in his company, he will tell the story of this remarkable individual.

———————

In all humility, both Ormond McGill and I had the inner conviction that the answers to many soul-searching questions would be ours when we journeyed deep into the East. Both of us had long looked forward to a trip to India, and now that we were there, we aimed to fully respond, both introspectively and objectively, by keeping our minds alert and our camera and pens constantly active recording that which we saw.

But perhaps I digress. We had hardly settled down in our hotel room at the Great Eastern of Calcutta when a tall bearer announced a caller.

202

"Show him in," I said.

Immediately, Sri U. C. Chakroborty was ushered into the room. He was dressed in the style of the Bengali, with a long colorless shirt that hung loosely and diaper-type pants that had characterized the attire of the late Mahatma Ghandi. His two hands literally floated up together and pressed palm to palm in authentic East Indian fashion as he greeted me. I noticed a garland of beautiful flowers that hung around his neck; the next thing I knew, he had removed the garland and had gently placed it around me.

"Thank you," I murmured softly.

"It is Indian custom. I hope you do not object."

"I like the custom," I responded, happily.

"I believe we have a mutual friend back in the United States," Sri Chakraborty queried, raising his eyebrows.

I knew he had reference to Mary Maier, a friend of long standing who had spent much time studying in India. It was she who had arranged this meeting.

"Yes," I replied, "but I think she calls you 'Nabagour'."

"That is my spiritual name."

Moments later, my partner in adventure, Ormond McGill, came in, and, after introductions, we all sat down and chatted quietly, our conversation covering a wide range of subjects dealing with India's religions and philosophy. I felt it fortunate that we had both spent some time studying these subjects prior to leaving on our trip.

"May heaven send you its richest blessing my sons, for I see you have both done exhaustive research in esoteric studies," Sri Chakraborty commented.

Mac and I glanced at each other. We honestly didn't feel that we deserved such credit, but we accepted it with a smile. We looked at this gentlemanly counterpart of Ghandi and nodded our appreciation.

"Will you join me in a *kirtan* Saturday?" he asked.

Chakraborty had pronounced it with a Bengali accent, "kee-tone," however, we knew what it represented—a religious song-fest of the Hindus, generally to some saint of significance. In this instance, it was in honor of Pravoo Jagadbandhu, who, to some eleven million Hindus that follow this specific sect, is the equivalent of what Jesus Christ is to the Christians.

Mac couldn't attend the *kirtan*, since he was playing his show at the Empire Theatre; nonetheless, I anticipated the song-fest with much interest when Sri Chakraborty and I entered the room and noted about thirty other devotees of Jagadbandhu, all seated around on the floor chanting and swaying their bodies rhythmically.

It was in this packed room that I first met Parimal Bandhu.

As I sat on the floor among the others, the jingling of cymbals

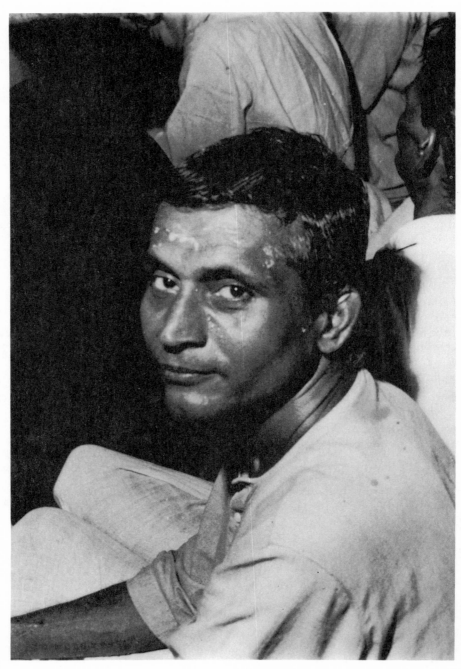

Sadhu Parimal Bandhu

and sharp percussion drums increased in tempo. *Why* I chose that particular place I shall never know, but seated immediately next to me was Sadhu Parimal Bandhu. He smiled almost angelically. I wanted to introduce myself, but even though talking was prohibited, it would have been next to impossible over the din of clapping hands and loud drum beats, for by now the noise had increased to a new high as the chanting Bengalis sang louder and louder with religious zeal.

Three hours later it was over. Sri Chakraborty advanced and gave Parimal Bandhu some *prashade*—a sacred food offered first to God before being consumed by human mouths. Sadhu pressed his hands palm to palm in acknowledgment of the food, then gingerly put it in my mouth. The stuff tasted sweet, almost too sweet, but I gulped it down and smiled, trying to show my appreciation. Apparently that was the correct thing to do, that is, as far as Indians are concerned, because moments later, it seemed, every hand in the room offered more *prashade* and I was the recipient.

Later that night I asked Sadhu, who walked me back to my hotel, whether he was a regular attendant to the *kirtan*. His reply came as a sort of shock.

"I come to the kirtans on occasions," he replied, "but this night I came because I was directed to."

That there is a wealth of superknowledge just beyond the border of our normal thoughts that can be aroused and commanded by some I have never doubted, but now I wondered if this chance meeting with Sadhu was really chance; I decided to inquire in this aspect.

"What do you mean, you were directed to?"

"Let me say for the moment," he put forth, "some inner impulse directed my actions—I knew that I would meet someone tonight who should be met, so I came forth and there you were."

The possibility that Parimal Bandhu had some other source of information of my going to the *kirtan* crossed my mind at the time, but later I came to learn that this man knew a great deal more than was ordinarily known, and *did* possess a mysterious faculty of foresight.

Whatever the affinity was I may never know, but Sadhu never left my side during my stay in India. Generally, he was the last person I saw at night before retiring, and usually the first person to greet me in the morning. And, because of the multiplicity of subjects related to the magical charm of India, which included everything from bathing in the Holy Ganges, fakir magic and snake-charming to visits to secret temples, I grew to depend on him for both counsel and spiritual unfoldment.

I asked Sadhu about Provoo Jagadbandhu, the Indian sage in

Parimal Bandhu and Ron Ormond with students of oriental religions.

whose honor the *kirtan* was held that evening when we met. He explained that, as with the Buddha, Jagadbandhu had lived the most humble of lives and in no way sought deification, but his life-example and reported miracles of healings and other supernormal phenomena were such as to gather a great following about him.

Sadhu's mention of "miracles of healings" greatly whetted my appetite for further knowledge, so I asked him for more information. Both Mac and I were greatly interested in the whole range of psychological and religious applications to the curing of disease. Having visited the great Shrine of Quiapo in the Philippines and other venerated healing centers in the Far East, we had a far more than average interest in these subjects, and I was most anxious to explore the methods of the yogis through the eyes of Parimal Bandhu. In this connection, I realized that healing of the sick in relation to religious practice is considered a power directly derived from God, or, as they prefer to refer to it in India, the God-source, and use it in a variety of ways according to many and diverse beliefs, i.e., by means of prayers, ceremonies, laying-on-of-hands, incantation, amulets, talismans, rings, relics, images, etc. We wondered what the modus operandi might be in India, where the practice of yoga is so predominent. The method of yoga consists in the controlling of the self, conscious as well as unconscious. What is called the "six-fold path of yoga" is held as a means to it. The first two, abstention and observation, refer to ethical preparation. The next two, posture and regulation of breath, insist on the discipline of the body to make it more flexible. The next step is the withdrawal of the senses from their natural outward function, while the last step along the path comes upon entering the state of *samadhi*, which is a vital element of yoga.

"Where might I find such a holy one who has such powers of healing," I asked Parimal Bandhu.

"I will show you that myself."

"You're a healer also?" I asked bluntly. "I was under the impression you were a philosopher and writer."

"The works of a *sadhu* are many and diverse," he said sympathetically. "While I do write, hoping to bring the eternal truth to humanity, I also have many who depend upon me for their spiritual needs. Healing is one of their needs."

The next morning when I awoke I unconsciously followed my custom. Slipping into my sarong-like pants, I walked to the door and opened it. There had been no knock, I simply knew Sadhu would be there. I wasn't wrong, for, as usual, he stood smiling.

"Come in," I greeted, then, glancing at my wristwatch, I noticed it was a full hour earlier than his usual morning arrival.

"You're early this morning."

"I have an appointment for you this morning."

"Good," I answered, "I'll shower and be with you in a few minutes."

It was during the act of soaping myself when the thought occurred. Why had I gotten up earlier than usual; there had been no knock, or appointment for that matter? I recalled the subject of telepathy, which I had discused with Parimal Bandhu some days before.

"Telepathy," he had said, "is primarily the communion of the subjective (spiritual) mind, or rather the normal means of communication between subjective minds. The reason of the apparent rarity of its manifestation is that exceptional conditions are required to bring its results above the threshold of consciousness. There is every reason to believe that our souls or subjective minds (as the Hindus use the term) can and do habitually hold communion with others when not the remotest perception of the fact is communicated to the objective intelligence. While this type of communion is not generally understood among men, it is assuredly an integral part of their lives."

When I got out of the shower I asked bluntly, "Then, when I was asleep, my objective mind allowed my subjective mind to accept your message that I awaken an hour earlier. Is that correct?"

"Practically," he came back. "Your subjective mind simply received my thoughts and at the precise moment you were to awaken, informed your objective mind—and you woke up!"

To say the least, I was impressed with Sadhu Parimal Bandhu. Not only did he talk about telepathy, he did something about it, and used it as an important part of his daily life, incorporating it into his remarkable practice of mental healing. McGill and I discussed at length his practical theories on yogi methods of health and healing; subjects which are as old as time and yet are as modern as tomorrow. Parimal Bandhu simply called it yoga. I usually refer to it as "yogi therapeutics." During our stay in India, Sadhu explained it while Mac took copious notes. These are presented in the next chapter.

To return to this reporting, "In speaking of yoga, as a healing talent," Sadhu stated, "With it everyone is a healer and can be remarkably helpful to others."

"It might be a little strange for us of the West," I said.

"It should not be," he rejoined. "Your great Master, Jesus, used it."

When I had finished dressing and shaving, I left a note for my partner telling him not to expect me until later.

Approximately thirty minutes after we had wound our way through the narrow streets of Calcutta, Sadhu paused in front of the door to a two-story, stucco-type residence. My eyes moved upward; I noted it was an old building. Then, through one of the windows, I saw several pairs of eyes looking down. I smiled cheerfully and waved an American style "hello." The heads as well as the eyes darted from view.

"We are in the neighborhood of the Doms," Sadhu spoke quietly.

I remembered reading about them; they are also known as the "untouchables," a kind of throw-back to the old caste system of India.

"The people we are going to see," I inquired, "are they Doms, and do they live in this building?"

"They are Doms and they do live in this building—but so do about ten other families."

He looked at me speculatively, probably to check my reaction. I smiled and said nothing. I was busily occupied now, watching a crowd of Hindus which had magically formed around us. They were quite harmless and jabbered rapidly in Bengali. I turned questioningly to Sadhu.

"They are speculating our connection," he explained.

A short while later the door opened and we both entered a small, dingy room clouded in semi-darkness. Laying prostrate on the floor was Sadhu's patient. His greeting, as well as the subsequent conversation, was in the native language, but Sadhu kept me filled in with an occasional remark. The woman on the floor was obviously ill, very ill. I tried to diagnose her case, but couldn't.

"Her lower limbs have been paralyzed for about three weeks," Sadhu said evenly.

"Has she seen a doctor?"

"Yes, and for that reason I could not come before; her son does not believe as we do, that she can be cured by yoga."

"Then why are we here now?"

"Because she sent for me last night."

"By messenger?"

Through meditation," he replied gently. "You see, the doctor says she will never walk again."

"Oh, and what do you say?"

"She will walk a little tomorrow."

When Sadhu dropped me off at the hotel he said he would not see me anymore that day or night, that he would go into meditation for the sick woman.

"I hope it makes her feel much better," I said, trying to console him.

"I have told her to sleep and that if she awakes, to pray. If she does that I can contact her mind by yoga, and heal. But like your Christ so aptly put it, she must also have faith."

The next morning Sadhu was at my door again, but unlike the previous day, he arrived at his usual time.

"How is the patient?" I greeted him.

"We shall go and see together."

When we arrived this time, a few less eyes were watching me, for by now I was no longer a novelty. When the door opened, Parimal Bandhu's patient greeted us. True, she had not fully recovered, nor was she as spry as a woman her age could be—but she was moving around on her own power; enough power to allow us to enter and later serve tea.

The more Mac and I came to know Parimal Bandhu, the more we appreciated his devotion to God and mankind. It must be admitted that the Hindu holy man was certainly far from being a Christian, but his loyalty to cause and humanity was unquestionably sublime.

While in India, and principally because of the Sadhu, Ron and I were able not only to observe but to actually participate with the Hindus in their private rites and ceremonies. Through his kind and always benevolent assistance, it became possible to become part of some incredible experiences and obtain information that a foreigner would ordinarily not be permitted entry into.

The sage, Sadhu Parimal Bandhu, at the kirtan.

Ron Ormond filming at the Jainist shrine.

17

Yoga (Yogi Therapeutics) in India

I have long been interested in gaining a better understanding of the so called "supernormal powers" of the yogi. Parimal Bandhu taught us many things, viz.:

The yogi, through rigid practices of self discipline, both mental and physical, have developed some unique abilities that are assuredly far enough above what one would call normal to be worthy of being considered super. They place particular emphasis upon the use of *Pranayama* (special breathing practices) in developing these superior powers. The yogi emphasize that in no sense are their practices to be considered supernatural, which represents powers above the range of nature, but that these unusual talents are to be regarded as perfectly normal virtues that every human has within his capacity.

I asked Sadhu about the yogi viewpoint on clairvoyance and astral projection.

He explained that the yogis hold that the mind can function on the astral plane in addition to that of ordinary physical existence. They say that the mind can come to employ "astral senses," rather than being limited by the five senses of the physical mind. Its object is to perceive, by these astral senses, what they call "associated astral images," rather than the actual physical objects of which these astral images are the counterparts.

Just what was meant by "astral image counterparts" was at first confusing to me, but it was explained that the view is held that all physical matter has, simultaneously, an astral as well as a physical existence. Thus, the astral perceptive power (clairvoyance) of the trained mind (seer) does not actually see the physical realities, but rather perceives the astral counterparts thereof.

To illustrate, in the yogi state, it is as if the astral plane were a great mirror in which is pictured the most minute details of all that occurs on the physical plane. This being so, the adept, having tuned his mind to function on the astral plane level, is able to discern this "associated astral image" of each and every thing or action occurring on the physical plane.

In clairvoyant perception and/or astral projection, space is not a limitation. In clairvoyant thought it is but necessary to think of a distant place or scene in order to be there on the astral plane, and to perceive the associated images of that place or scene. Thus, the yogi explain, although the physical body of the clairvoyant observer remains in its original place on the physical or material plane, his thought is able to project itself on the astral plane to any desired point in space (astral projection), and, once there, is able to see astrally, by means of the "astral senses," all the events occurring at that place.

I asked about these astral senses. The Sadhu continued his explanation. The yogi teach that man has, in addition to the five physical senses, i.e., seeing, hearing, feeling, smelling, and tasting, the corresponding astral counterparts of these, which, while largely dormant in most people, may be rendered active through the practice of *Pranayama*. In clairvoyance and astral projection, the initiate penetrates the veil of the astral plane, and there perceives the counterparts of physical happening through the use of the astral counterparts of his senses.

I am indebted to Parimal Bandhu for this material relative to Yogi methods of healing, health and well-being. There is oriental wisdom here—a contribution from the East to the West. I write in the oriental vein precisely as the Sadhu passed on this information while standing at my side.

The Initiates of the East have considerable philosophical differences from their western brothers in beliefs and methods of health and healing. These are the basic yogi methods of bringing health through the powers of the mind. They are referred to as "practices of yoga." In India, these practices are considered as positive in their application as are the methods of the occidental physician; however, as an American, I fully appreciate that the cultures of East and West see things through very different eyes.

The oriental healer accepts an intimate relationship between the mind and body, and between mental states and physical conditions. Their point-of-view is in no sense fanatical, for the Yogis do not hold that physical ailments are purely imaginary and that disease is "all in the mind," nor, conversely, do they believe that mental healing methods are worthless. Theirs is a belief in the treatment of disease through a balance of both the physical and the mental.

The principle to be understood in the practice of "yogi therapeutics" is the conception that the processes of the physical body are vital activities governed and directed by the mind. And, in the treatment of disease by Yoga processes, it is to be understood that this is not treatment of mind upon the body directly, but is treatment of mind upon mind.

There is life in every part, every organ, every cell of the body; life-force is present wherever life abides. And wherever life and life-forces are present, there are also mind and mental-forces present. Life always indicates mind; likewise, mind always indicates life.

The above being accepted as true, the Yogi holds that every organ and cell of the body has mind in it; the human body is thus appreciated as being mental in its inner nature, rather than a mere physical machine. By that is not implied that the body is not a physical machine and that it has not mechanical and chemical action, but along with this it is held that these mechanical and chemical actions are capable of being placed under the control and direction of certain parts of the mind. This is the practice of yoga, what Ron elected to call yogi therapeutics.

When I speak of mind in its application for the curing of disease, understand that I do not refer to the phase of mind known as conscious. This, we know, has little effect in "running the body." Rather, I speak of the subconscious phases of mind, which are in direct contact with and are important to regulating the processes of the body. Subconscious is a western term, but I employ it for the reader's ready comprehension. By this appreciation, you will begin to understand the oriental belief that a phase of mind is present in every part of the body, and the importance of the concept of the effect of mind upon mind as the functioning process of yogi therapeutics— for the subconscious phase of mind controls the operation of every organ, part, and cell of the body. This part of the mind never sleeps; it is ever tending its duties, i.e., the constant work of repair, replacement, change, digestion, assimilation, elimination, etc. All these functions are continually performed by the subconscious, completely below the threshold of consciousness. It is the Yogi's belief that the basic power of mental healing lies in the controlling and directing toward the desired ends of the cure the powers invested in the subconscious phase of mind, which in turn manifests the correction of the disease and the causing of the body to function as it should.

Oriental healers hold the belief that each cell of the body possesses a micro-brain of its own, and in the blending of various cells together to form, let us say, an organ, produces yet a higher form of brain innate to the organ. It is in response to the higher commands of the subconscious phase of mind that these rudimentary brains respond. This is the mechanism upon which healings by yoga operate.

Also in the practice of yoga (yogi therapeutics), I will give attention to controlling aspects. Seven factors of health essentials are maintained:

1. Healthy eating
2. Healthy drinking
3. Healthy breathing
4. Healthy exercise and rest
5. Healthy air and sunshine
6. Healthy elimination
7. Healthy thinking

These are essential to the promotion of health; I will consider each in turn.

1. HEALTHY EATING.

The ultimate fate of the food we eat is its assimilation into the blood. The blood has been rightly called "liquid flesh," for this nourishing fluid substance is carried in circulation to all parts of the body to exactly where it is needed to feed every cell. Thus, it is said, "the blood is the life."

The above being a truism, the choice of food that we place in our body, that in turn enters the blood that feeds all tissues, is of great importance.

The first step in healthy food assimilation is careful mastication. It is here that the process of healthy eating begins. For health, chew well, mixing the saliva thoroughly in the process before allowing the food to enter the stomach. There is chemical action there for healthy assimilation and digestion.

Remember this rule well: give your digestive cells the kind of food material that nature intended them to have—material properly masticated and insalivated. The Yogi's method of food mastication is to *deliberately* (while thinking of the food, not allowing mind distraction in the process of eating) chew all food so completely that it is reduced to a soft pulp, which gradually "swallows itself" without conscious effort. Any remainder of food that is not so automatically swallowed is removed from the mouth as waste product and is discarded. By this method, it becomes possible to subsist in full health, strength, and weight upon a small fraction of the food that the ordinary man consumes when not utilizing such careful methods of mastication, as every particle of the nourishment is thus extracted from the food. The words of the Yogi express the principle thus: "Chew all food thoroughly, until it dissolves itself and is swallowed involuntarily by you; at the same time hold in your mind the thought that you are extracting from the food that *Prana* (an oriental term for the energy all-pervading in the Universe) which nature has placed in it, and which has caused it to grow and develop in its natural state. The right thought, added to the right mastication, tends to release and unloose the particles of *Prana,* and to cause you to absorb them into your system. This is the whole secret of the yogi method of healthy eating that is passed to you."

Another point of healthy eating, as practiced in yogi therapeutics, is the developing of the habit of eating in response to hunger instead of appetite. Hunger is the feeling denoting the normal demand of the system for food. Appetite, on the other hand, is the abnormal, cultivated craving for the taste of certain foods. Whenever food is needed in the system, the subconscious mind will announce the need by the sensation of hunger. Learn to distinguish between genuine hunger and the gnawing sensations caused by unnatural appetite. Hunger is never a disagreeable feeling accompanied by weakness or gnawing feelings of the stomach; it is a pleasant anticipatory desire for food, and is felt mostly in the mouth and throat. It comes only when the subconscious perceives that the body is ready to receive, digest, and assimilate food.

The Yogi is rarely concerned with particular diet, as it is held that with the regulated body the subconscious phase of mind will automatically select, in response to hunger, those foods especially needed. In general, the yogi avoids "man-made dishes" and rich foods, and stresses the eating of natural foods.

Yoga advocates: "Mix good thoughts with good food as you eat your way to health."

2. Healthy drinking.

Next to food in importance in the maintenance of good health is drinking. The subconscious mind directs the body to respond to the need for water by the development of sensations of thirst. This is a basic craving, and here again one must distinguish between artificial thirst appetite and real thirst hunger.

There are actually only three natural fluids for the real satisfying of thirst: water, fruit juices, and milk. These are named in the order of their importance. All other thirst-quenching liquids are purely acquired appetites, and are not recommended. Natural thirst is invariably satisfied with water, particularly with water of an agreeable temperature.

Water in the body is essential to health. It is needed as fluid material for the blood. It is needed in the manufacture and secretion of the various chemical fluids and juices of the body. If there are not sufficient fluids in the system for other purposes, nature draws upon the fluids of the blood and thus robs it. Water, also, performs an important function in the process of the elimination of waste products from the body. It is also essential to breathing, heat control, and other vital processes.

The importance of water in the human system is obvious from this dissertation. How much water does yoga recommend for good health? The answer is very direct: not less than two quarts of water must be drunk every twenty-four hours. Man in his healthful state will instinctively drink at least this amount. The water should not be drunk all at one time, but rather taken several times a day in moderate amounts. A glass of water when first arising and just before retiring is a good policy to start and end the day. The only "don't" in regard to drinking water is not to drink it during periods when you are masticating food. This does not mean you cannot drink water with your meals, but simply do not use it to wash down your foods.

In drinking water, never gulp it down. Let it remain in the mouth a moment before you swallow it. The yogi claim that this process, combined with the holding of the proper thought, provides you the means of extracting full *Prana* from the water. This, of course, western readers will appreciate as an eastern concept.

3. HEALTHY BREATHING.

In his natural state, man needs no special instructions for this third element of healthy living. However, in some cases, harmful habits of breathing have been acquired and must be corrected. Breathing is the most vital of physical processes for the maintenance of life, in the supplying of the blood with oxygen and performing a variety of important chemical processes throughout the body. Without breath there is no life. The rules of healthy breathing are simple. First, remember to breathe through your nostrils and not through your mouth. This is an essential to health. Warmed and filtered air is demanded by nature; the nostrils exactly provide this. If one's habits of breathing are wrong, then they must be corrected. One of the best ways is to deliberately realize the natural functions of the lungs and the importance of breathing right, and secondly visualize the idea of the habit of right breathing performed by yourself. Once the conscious mind gets this idea fixed in itself, the subconscious gradually adopts the habit of performing the act of breathing in the correct and natural way, instead of in the imperfection that has been forced upon it by neglect and bad habits. A correct carriage of the shoulders and chest enables the subconscious to perform this action more readily. Get the mental picture right, the physical carriage right, and nature will do the rest automatically.

An excellent exercise in this practice of yoga is expressed, "Keep yourself straight and breathe deeply. Let the mental conception of one's self be held in the mind. Instantly expand the chest, throw back the shoulders and straighten up. Then draw in the breath until the lungs are filled to their utmost capacity, and while holding it for an instant in the lungs, throw the shoulders back still further and stretch the chest; at the same time try to pull the spine forward between the shoulders. Then let the air go out easily."

What the Yogi call "the complete breath" is also a wonderful exercise. To perform this, stand or sit erect. Breathe through the nostrils and inhale steadily, first filling the lower part of the lungs, which exerts a gentle pressure on the abdominal organs and pushes forward the front walls of the abdomen. Then fill the middle part of the lungs, pushing out the lower ribs, breastbone and chest. Next fill the higher part of the lungs, protruding the upper chest, thus lifting the chest, including the upper six or seven pairs of ribs. In the final movement, the lower part of the abdomen will be slightly drawn in, this movement giving the lungs a support and also helping to fill the higher part of the lungs. The entire exercise is performed in one continuous inhalation; the entire chest to the highest point in the region of the collarbone being expanded with a uniform movement. Avoid a jerky series of inhalations and strive to acquire a steady, continuous breath.

Now, retain the breath a few moments; then exhale quite slowly, holding the chest in a firm position and drawing the abdomen in a little and lifting it upward slowly as the air leaves the lungs. When the air is entirely exhaled, relax the chest and abdomen. A little practice will render this part of the exercise easy, and the movement, once acquired, will be afterwards performed almost automatically.

Visualize yourself in a mental picture of breathing properly as a settled habit. Supply the right pattern and the subconscious phase of mind will do the rest. The Yogi hold that *Prana* enters and charges the body more via the breath than through any other process.

4. HEALTHY EXERCISE AND REST.

This is the fourth of the seven yogi health essentials. Nature intends that man shall exercise his body. Exercise produces muscular contraction in which the blood is propelled, carrying with it the wasted, worn-out material. And when the contraction is relaxed, fresh blood from the arteries flows into the muscles, carrying with it fresh building material, fresh oxygen and energy. The activity of exercise thus stimulates all the functions of the body.

Yoga holds that for exercise to be beneficial, the mind must be thrown into the exercising process as well. Mere physical exercise without this important factor is not enough. It is a truth that the circulation follows the attention. The Yogi method of mind-physical exercise is by this process: Whatever the physical method of exercise the person engages in, be it planned calisthenics, walking, swimming, athletics, etc., simultaneous with such activity, always send mind to the desired part by willing concentrated energy there, coupled with the firm belief and faith that it will do so, and give to this a positive form by the mental-picture of the desired results from the exercise being obtained.

This is very important, so I will explain by example. Suppose you are exercising your chest, shoulders, and arm muscles. As you go through the physical exercises, at the same time, mentally picture yourself as gaining in strength and physical perfection as you wish to be. This plan converts a "dead" system of exercise into a living series of actions. It is vital to well being.

Yogi therapeutic does not present any especial exercises other than to generally state that each person work out his own regimen to his personal advantage, following the general principle that all such exercises stretch and then contract each muscle, part, or limb, while keeping in mind the words (and their accompanying actions) stretch, contract, twist, bend, wiggle, shake. By doing this, you will work out a good system for yourself.

The yogi recommend "shaking yourself," an action akin to that performed by a big dog when he shakes from his hide the water after a swim. By observing the bending, twisting, stretching, wiggling, shaking, crouching, and crawling of the animals, you will get all the pointers you need in the developing of instinctive exercises for health.

Resting, in its own way, is as important to body health as is exercise, for without it physical culture is incomplete. Muscular relaxation has powerful effects upon the nerves, feelings, emotions, and brain. Yoga stresses this importance for preserving health and strength, and teaches a philosophy of relaxation based upon the example of the cat family, i.e., lions, tigers, leopards, etc. The student is bid study the attitude of a cat in repose; use the cat as your model, and hold the thought of it when you wish to relax your body thoroughly.

In resting, endeavor to relax completely. Take the tension off the mind and the nerves as well as the muscles. Take your mind off of your muscles and just let go. Picture yourself as being heavy as lead and dropping of your own weight onto the bed or chair; think of yourself as being limp as a wet cloth. Picture yourself as withdrawing all nervous force from every voluntary muscle and allow yourself to remain limp and apparently lifeless from head to toe.

You can doze at the same time, if you wish, or remain wide awake with the senses keen and alert but with muscles completely relaxed and body limp. One hour of such rest will refresh you as much as a whole night's sleep refreshes the average man.

5. HEALTHY AIR AND SUNSHINE.

To the man or woman leading a natural life in the open, little need be said on this important fifth principle of yoga for healthy living. But so many people today live such an abnormal, shut-in life that special attention must be given to it.

Nature has provided two great gifts for the well-being of her children in air and sunshine. These must be taken advantage of.

Fresh air supplies life-giving oxygen to the lungs and allows the burning of waste matter in the system. In the open air, this supply is normal. For this reason, always allow plenty of ventilation about yourself whenever possible. Make it your deliberate practice to get plenty of fresh air. Plan a brisk walk in the open air, and keep out in the open air as much as possible. And remember, fresh air is needed at night as well as during the day.

Nature also intended her children to have the benefit of sunshine. But it must be a natural process, not one of deliberate overexposure. Sunbaths that "cook" one in the sun are definitely not the way. Indeed, overexposure to sunlight is harmful. But used with intelligence and with care, it provides wonderful therapy. Just being out-of-doors in the fresh air and sunlight, keeping the head covered so the face may be in shade, has excellent benefits. Use air and sunlight naturally. The virtue of sunshine lies not in the heat of the sun, but rather in the light, which has a chemical action on the skin and body.

The Yogis teach that the *Prana* in the sunshine is absorbed by the body, bringing new energy and life. There are elements in the light from the sun that pass directly through the skin and are absorbed by the blood.

For health, plan your living so your rooms may be well-sunned and well-aired. Flood your rooms with sunlight at least once a day. Let it shine upon you when out-of-doors, particularly in the early morning. But remember, use it wisely and in moderation. Too much of a good thing can be bad. "Let a little sunshine in" is a good rule to follow, and "Let a little sunshine fall upon me" is a good twin-rule to observe.

6. HEALTHY ELIMINATION.

Without the successful performance of this function, which is en-

tirely regulated by the subconscious mind and its associated controlled cells and cell-groups, health is impossible. The body's waste
products are removed from the system through the breath, through
the skin, through the kidneys, and through the bowels. The smooth
functioning of these processes is absolutely essential. One of the most
common difficulties in this regard is constipation. Yogi therapeutics
has developed methods for such correction: 1. Increasing the amount
of fluids partaken daily. 2. Adding a little roughage to the food,
such as bran, in order to stimulate the secretions of fluids by the
intestines. 3. Exercising the abdominal muscles by alternate contraction and expansion. 4. Applying the methods and principles of
healthy thinking, which I will next discuss.

7. HEALTHY THINKING.

This seventh and last of the seven yogi health essentials intro-
duces an element of health that is of great interest to the student
of psychology, viz., that one's feelings, emotions and general mental
states are reflected and materialized in his physical condition. In
other words, the mental attitude of the individual is seen to have
much to do with his state of health. Bright, cheerful and happy
mental attitudes reflect themselves in the normal functioning of the
physical body, while the mental states of depression, gloom, worry,
fear, hate, jealousy, and anger all react upon the body to produce
abnormal functioning.

In western terminology, such mental and/or emotional states
that cause physical harm to the body are known as psychosomatic.
Such conditions are surprisingly common, and it can be correctly
stated that a considerable proportion of both acute and chronic disease—both functional and organic—are caused by the mental states of
the person, and may be cured by a reversal of those mental states.
Yoga has held this belief and performed such cures for centuries,
and looks upon many diseases, to a major extent, as being due to
mental causes, and, as such, holds that these diseases may be cured
by mental powers.

In both mental cause and mental cure, however, it should be understood by the student that the cure is produced through the effect
of mental states upon the physiological processes; the physiological
processes, themselves, it must be remembered, are largely "mental"
in nature, being animated and energized by means of the life and
mind in organs, cells and cell-groups, and being under the general
control and direction of the subconscious mind.

Sadhu was warming to his subject, this mental-curing aspect being very close to his interests. Before he proceeded further, though,
I raised a hand and asked the question, "Can you give me some ad-

ditional insight into this *Prana* that seems present in the application of all seven of these Yogi essentials to health?"

Parimal Bandhu answered immediately: "*Prana* is the sum-total of all force in the universe, mental and physical. We hold that the force that puts all nature into operation and keeps it in operation is *Prana*. The knowledge and control of *Prana* is what is called *Pranayama*. The master, having achieved *Pranayama*, has nature under his control. When the ignorant see these powers they call them miracles. He who has grasped *Prana* has grasped all the powers and forces of the universe. It is free energy. *Prana* is the generalized manifestation of force.

"In relation to yogi therapeutics, the practices are such as to bring in *Prana*. Western people never seem to grasp the tremendous truth that the power, the force, the energy is a great reservoir *outside* that must be drawn within the man. Once tapped and drawn upon it may be used and controlled by the mind for whatever purpose is desired, as it is an impartial force. Thus, you will observe that the methods of yoga are not methods of health for themselves alone, but are designed in their practice to increase the flow of *Prana*, that it may be utilized toward the ends of healing and good health."

I raised my hand again; somehow I felt like a schoolboy. "That is enough. I have my answer as far as I can grasp it at the moment. Please continue with your discussion of yoga, or as Ron terms it, yogi therapeutics."

I continue to write from his comments.

As has been observed, yoga in relation to therapy is not the action of mind upon matter, but rather that of mind upon mind. More explicitly, it is not a case of mind producing an effect upon matter, but rather, of one kind (or phase) of mind producing an effect upon another kind of mind within the body, while *Prana* provides the needful energy.

Yogi therapeutics holds that all mental causes of disease and all mental cures of disease may be reduced to the one fundamental truth, namely, that the mental principle operative in cause and cure of disease is that of mental image plus belief. Mental image and belief constitute the operative mental state serving to account for both the mental cause of disease and the mental curing of disease.

In all cases of the mental cause and cure of disease it will be found invariably, first, the idea or mental picture, or similar representation of some thing, event, or condition connected with some pleasant or unpleasant feeling or emotion concerning the thing pictured in the mind. In short, it may be the idea-picture of something that may happen to yourself or to others in whom you are interested, or else it may be the idea-picture of some physical condition, desirable or undesirable, which may possibly happen to human beings. This idea-picture is the seed from which the physical condition develops.

Secondly, there is always found the mental element of belief, which gives power and effect to the "seed-idea," above mentioned. Belief can be defined as acceptance of a fact, faith, credence, trust, reliance, or assurance. Faith, hope, fear, dread, and expectation are all forms of belief. The forms of belief which are particularly active in the mental cause and cure of disease are those which may be grouped into two general classes, i.e., hope, in some degree or form, and fear, in some degree or form.

Hope and fear are almost identical in essential principle, though working in opposite directions. Hope is the desire for something good, and the expectation of good occurrence; fear is the apprehension of impending danger and the expectation of evil or harmful occurrence. Midway between hope and fear may sometimes be found a form of feeling called "simple belief," or expectation based upon opinions of happenings neither good nor evil. In hope, fear, and simple belief there is always present the active element of expectation, i.e., looking forward to as likely to happen or become, with anticipation based on belief in the happening. This expectation is the energizing element which makes the "seed-idea" develop into physical form.

With this understanding of the basic cause and cure of disease as an active manifestation of mind, we are now ready to consider that phase of yoga which deals with the practice of mental healing.

The fundamental secret of mental healing is the creation and maintenance of the right mental image of the normal condition desired and the arousing and maintenance of the right beliefs, i.e., faith, confidence, anticipation, and expectation of the realization of the desired results.

Upon the above formula rest all the various methods and systems of mental healing. The rest is purely a matter of applying the mental force thus aroused, and of following the most efficient methods of directing it.

In presenting the yogi techniques of healing, I shall commence by pointing out first the methods to be applied in what is called "autohealing"—the healing of one's self.

It is first necessary to cultivate the art of forming clear and strong visualization of mental pictures or mental images. This requires the use of the will applied in concentrated attention, and the imagination faculty of the mind applied in forming the mental image. The reason for the cultivation of this art is that your mental image of the desired physical condition is the mold for the materialization of the physical condition; the picture of the desired condition must first exist in your mind before it can be reproduced in your physical organism through the process of being first deliberately established in the conscious mind, following which the subconscious appropriates the ideal-picture and establishes it in its own field of operations.

It is a three step process: 1. You create the mental image in your conscious mind. 2. Your subconscious accepts the ideal and establishes it below the level of consciousness. 3. The subconscious phase of mind and its associated cell-minds and organ-minds proceed to build and operate the physical organism in accordance with the ideal "working plan" which has been provided it in the form of your mental-picture or ideal.

Western students will probably not lean toward the practice, but those of the East frequently make use of the crystal ball as a powerful means of forming the mental-pictures; it is a wonderful aid in concentrating and forming strong visualizations, which are, in turn, taken over by the subconscious.

Nature has originally placed in the subconscious mind the right mental patterns. As you practice this art of mental healing you will experience an "instinctive knowledge" and will begin to feel beyond doubt that mind has direct influence over the body and is able to work on it for your good. There is a dynamic power to mental healing that is innate in life; as you visualize health and well-being and charge it with belief you will shortly begin to feel new powers of health buoyant within you.

Here is what is called "The General Treatment of Yoga (Yogi Therapeutics)": Relax and visualize strongly to yourself (or else use the crystal ball) a mental picture of yourself enjoying perfect health and normal physical condition. See yourself, in your visualizing-reverie, as experiencing the perfect manifestation of the "seven life essentials of yoga," as have been explained. See yourself manifesting right eating, right drinking, right exercise and rest, right air and sunshine, right elimination, and, above all, right thinking—thinking along the line of health rather than of disease; of faith rather than of fear. Then energize and animate these thought-pictures by full belief!

There is, also, a supplemental method of Yoga healing technique that can be applied for the correction of trouble or disease in any particular part of the body, that may be used in addition to the general treatment described, and that is "talking up to" the diseased part. To western students this may seem strange, but in the Orient it is recognized therapeutic practice.

In this procedure, talk to the organ or part of the body that is functioning improperly, just as you would to a disobedient child. The nearer you come to considering and treating the organ or part as if it were an actual entity or person the better will be its response to your treatment; for there is mind in the organ, part, or group of cells, and you are reaching out to it.

The best way to reach the mind of the cells is to command it to respond just as you would command an actual person. You must remonstrate, argue, coax, order, or drive the "person" residing in the organ, just as you would an individual. You may either talk aloud to the organ or you may talk to it mentally. Tell it just what you expect of it; just what you intend it to do; just what is right for it to do, etc. And it will obey you!

The "minds" in organs and parts of the body are decidedly similar to the minds of children, and, when affected, can often be unreasonably stubborn. But if they are reached after the right way, in a kindly but firm manner and tone, in most cases they will obey readily and mend their ways. Treat the organ as if it had an actual personality. Even go so far as to call it by name, as for instance, "here stomach-mind" or "listen to me liver-mind," etc. Sometimes a patting of the hand over the affected part seems to awaken the attention of the mind within it; after securing this attention, you may proceed with your treatment in the way just mentioned.[1]

I will proceed now to a consideration of various yoga methods for the healing of particular complaints. In general, these may be classified as disorders of the circulation, disorders of nutrition, and disorders of elimination. Most all chronic disorders have one or more of these factors prominent in the difficulty.

DISORDERS OF THE CIRCULATION

No organ of the body can perform its functions properly when the blood supplied to it is insufficient. On the other hand, many disorders are caused by stagnant circulation, with resulting congestion, etc. Yogi therapeutics has purposeful methods designed to equalize the circulation. Yoga healing is particularly efficacious in performing this work, since the circulation of the blood is especially amenable to voluntary or involuntary control and direction by the mind.

Remember this rule, blood circulation follows the attention, and the method of application is to lie down in a quiet place and take

---

1. This subject of personalizing the mind in the cells and conversing (commanding) them directly is a most interesting yoga concept. Western psychologists to whom I have spoken seem to feel the method is a means of giving suggestions to the subconscious. However, the yogi do not feel this way about it at all. They regard these "little minds" as true entities within their bodies which they can direct. Whatever the causation, the efficacy of the method is strongly testified to in the Orient.

the tension off every muscle. First, just let your mind idle for a few moments to remove all tension, and then develop your mental-picture and hold firmly this picture of the blood flowing freely, regularly, and naturally to all parts of the body, from head to foot, nourishing and energizing every part and portion thereof. At the same time, speak mentally to your subconscious mind in the blood and its organs, bidding it gently and kindly to attend properly to the work of equalizing circulation. Breathe easily and deeply, and with each inhalation think to yourself, "I am breathing in oxygen which will serve to stimulate and energize every cell, every organ, every part of my body; I am sending this energizing and vitalizing power to every part of my system, in an equalized circulation, giving to every part exactly what it needs."

Make a mental picture of the inflow of oxygen and energy, and of its distribution to each part of your body. You will become conscious of a decided increase of warmth in the body during this treatment.

In the event of pain in any part of the body, you should send an increased current of blood to the affected part, visualizing it as washing away the stagnant accumulations there, energizing and generally freshening it. The idea of inhaling the curative energy and exhaling the painful condition, held in thought as a mental picture, will be found helpful in such cases.

DISORDERS OF NUTRITION

The body depends for health and vigor upon proper nutrition. Many body weaknesses are directly or indirectly due to malnutrition. For the correction of such difficulties, the first thing to do is to "get right" with the first of the "seven health essentials of yoga"—the essential of healthy eating. Do this and you have accomplished fully half of the necessary work of the cure. The remainder is simply a matter of directing the organs of nutrition to resume the natural performance of their functioning, and to "forget" the slipshod, imperfect habits which have been forced upon them. The precise technique of the process is to recline in quiet repose, rest the mind, and then strongly visualize your body as functioning perfectly with the organs of digestion and assimilation performing their work properly, and of extracting every portion of nourishment from the good food you will feed it. Express the faithful expectation that the mental picture you are so forming will materialize in reality. At the same time, accompany this by verbal commands to the organs of digestion and assimilation to do their work properly. Tell them that you expect them to do their work well; that they are able to do their proper functioning, and that you expect them to do it. The commands to the stomach and intestinal minds should be friendly but firm; those to the liver-mind should be strong and commanding. And then apply this verbal affirmation: "I am sending a strong current of thought-force to my organs of digestion and assimilation, and am thus building them up and causing them to function as they should for perfect health. I have the true hunger of a healthy person. My stomach is able to digest every particle of food that I send into it, and it knows that I will send nothing into it that is not right. I will assimilate every particle of nourishment extracted from my food. I will extract every particle of strength from every ounce of food eaten and digested by me. I am developing strong digestive and assimilative powers. My organs of nutrition are becoming strong, stronger, stronger every day in every way. They are doing their work well, well, well, everyday in every way."

This form of treatment, accompanied, of course, by right eating, right drinking, right breathing, and right elimination, will tend to relieve and correct digestive and nutritional difficulties.

DISORDERS OF ELIMINATION

Without proper elimination there cannot be perfect health. When the "seven health essentials of yoga" are applied little else will be found necessary in the way of special treatment, as the matter of proper elimination of waste products from the body will be automatically taken care of. In the event of the need for special treatment for constipation, however, some special instructions will be valuable.

The mental element of the treatment of constipation is important, as it is a difficulty that becomes readily subject to habit. For its correction, in addition to using the "seven health essentials of yoga," recline quietly and visualize the colon and other parts concerned with bowel-excretion as doing their work properly; performing their functions naturally and normally as nature intended them to do. Carry this thought and mental picture with you, energized by faith and expectation of the desired results. Talk to the mind in those special parts, expressing regret at your neglect and promising proper attention in the future, and asking the mind in the parts to help and cooperate with you and to do its work properly. At the same time, give some special attention to the sphincter-anus muscle at the outer opening of the rectum by concentrating on it the thought and mental picture expressed by the word, "relax!" In fact, the whole treatment there should be the thought and mental picture of the parts relaxing, for the wrong habit and idea of contraction must be neutralized and overcome.

Also with this mental aspect of the treatment, you must increase your fluids by healthy drinking. You must mix a little bran or similar roughage in your food. You must exercise the abdominal muscles by alternate expansion and contraction—first "drawing in" and then "letting go out." Finally, you must "make an appointment with your bowels" (the mind in your bowels). Strange as it may appear to you, you can speedily get the bowels back into natural habits by fixing a certain convenient time in the morning and then conscientiously keeping the appointment. Before long, you will have "set" the new habit; after that keep the appointment regularly each morning, letting nothing prevent you from doing so. Let nature see that you are "making good," and she will do her best to "make good" likewise.

Here are some additional yogi therapeutic treatments for special complaints:

FEMALE DISORDERS

Such complaints are usually based upon imperfect methods of living in violation of some of the "seven health essentials of yoga." For their correction it follows that the first thing to be done is for the woman to get back into the pathway of correct living in the following of these principles. In general, a healthy woman seldom suffers from generative organ difficulties. If she does, building up general health by right living and right thinking will soon correct her special weaknesses. So, I repeat, let the woman suffering from female complaints begin by treatment for more general trouble, and correct her difficulties by following the "seven health essentials of yoga."

In cases of painful menstruation, I know of no better preliminary treatment than a combination of the treatment for disorders of the disgestion coupled with the increase of fluids and general treatment for female difficulties in general. Let the woman lie down in quiet and visualize clearly and plainly the desired healthy condition and activities of her organs that she desires. She must form a clear and positive mental image of herself as functioning normally in the natural way. She must hold before her subconscious mind the firmly fixed idea of her generative organs being just what they should be, and acting just as they should act. She should verbally instruct the mind in those organs to manifest the condition of health, strength, and normality.

She will find in her practice of the treatments that irregular menstruation is very amenable to mental commands. For these, she should fix her mind upon the day upon which her menstrual period should occur—beginning about three weeks ahead of that time, and then each day she should think about that time, making the affirmation that at that stated time her menstruation will begin. She should keep a calendar in her room, and upon it she should mark off day after day as it passes, keeping the expectant attention fixed upon the appointed date. At the same time, she should talk to the mind of the organ concerned with this work, telling it that she is trusting it to perform its work properly, and is expecting it to bring about the desired results. This treatment will, in most cases, bring about the desired results upon the exact date.

All of these treatments by mental means must be gone into with complete feelings of faith, hope, belief, confidence, and earnest expectation of the desired results occurring. Once energized, the body's response to such treatment is in truth remarkable.

MISCELLANEOUS COMPLAINTS

As Parimal Bandhu commented to us, there are, of course, multitudes of complaints that have not been specifically named in his discourse on yoga. He mentioned that the great majority of these will be found belonging in the general classification "miscellaneous," and may be affected by the treatments I have described. The cures are usually to be found in the observance of the "seven health essentials of yoga," plus the special methods of treatment which I have given of forming and holding the mental image of the healthy, normal functioning of the natural condition desired. Talking to the minds of the affected organs and parts and the feelings of faith, hope, confidence, and expectation constitute the essence and gist of the special mental treatment of ills by the method of yoga (yogi therapeutics).

ON HEALING OTHERS BY YOGA

When you have learned to heal yourself, you may then heal others by the application of the same general principles of self-healing that have been given. Indeed, you may even attempt some such mental cures prior to your own complete curing, as it is not uncommon for the healer in exerting the influence for a cure over a patient to find to his delight that he has effected the same cure in himself; as the strong mental images and ideals of the desired condition for the patient arouses such a strong faith and expectation and confidence in his mind, that it produces the desired effect upon his own body simultaneously.

The treatment of other persons by the method of Yoga follows exactly the same line as that employed in the case of self-treatment, as I have mentioned. The patient is requested to place himself in a relaxed condition; removing all tension from mind and body. He is requested to make his mind as passive and receptive to the words and thoughts of the healer as is possible. The healer, having first induced in himself the mental attitude of concentrated visualization, then proceeds to direct to the patient the words and thoughts, the mental-ideals and patterns, which he would direct to his own subconscious mind, and the mind in the organs and parts of his own body, in self-treatment. He should, also, prepare the mind of the patient by a short description of the "seven health essentials of yoga," pointing out the value of each. He should hold in his mind the mental image and ideal of the perfect, normal, healthy condition, and then "project" this into the mind of the patient by means of his words and concentrated thought.

The general rule for the healing of others by the yogi method is: Treat the patient just as you would treat yourself. The general and special treatments given in this discourse on yogi procedure of self-treatment should be applied to the patient in precisely the same way. Always commence your treatment of others by a strong visualization, in which you see the patient as receiving and being benefited by the treatment, and his body responding by becoming healthy and normal. In this visualization, the healer should see himself, also, as positive, strong, dynamic, and filled with the mental healing power. To this add the element of faith, confidence, and expectation of the desired cure occurring. So prepared, be assured of this fact: that you will effect the cure and proceed with confidence and positive expectation of the desired healing.

I recall, at the time of my taking these notes on yogi therapeutics from Parimal Bandhu's dictation in India, of my commenting on how very different were these healing methods of the yogi from those used by people of my own country. He merely shrugged and said, "The use of these methods is ages old."

As I complete this writing, I can still see Sadhu's bland, gentle smile before me. He was the most mild-mannered man Ron Ormond and I have ever known, yet he led Ron (with his own willingness, of course) into the most eerie experience of his life. I will tell of this adventure in the next chapter.

A holy man of India.

A visit to the banks of the holy Ganges River.

The power of faith displayed in India.

Alms for the sacred monkeys of India.

A sacred cow in India. This one has its keeper. Many "sacred cows" roam about the streets of the cities unattended. They are greatly venerated.

18

The Sacred Room
of Provoo Jagadbandhu

Ron and I had come a long way in search of what was here directly before us, one of the hallowed religious sanctuaries of the Orient. The last lap of the journey on foot down the back alleys of Calcutta had been most exciting. We were deep in the domain of the Doms —the "untouchables" of India, at a spot where it is doubtful that any white man (let alone an American) had ever knowingly come before, for this was the Holy of Holies of these outcast people. This was the sacred room of Jagadbandhu.

The usually noisy group of Bengali were strangely silent. The door to the room loomed before us. It was a small door, not more than a couple of feet wide by four feet high. It gaped a hole of darkness in the seamy plaster wall. Our eyes moved upward over the dirty face of the wall, onto the tops of the dingy buildings, and up to the darkening sky high above. It was an old building that we faced, not old in the sense of being ancient, since Calcutta is not that venerable a city, but old in that every vestige of newness was gone.

We looked at the group about us. The Hindus have an almost magical way of forming a crowd. Where, upon our arrival at the sacred spot, a dozen or so had been standing about, now there were at least a hundred. Their faces were taut, and the look in their eyes didn't make us feel any too happy either, as we realized that we trod on what to them was hallowed ground. Actually, we had no right to be here, other than the right of a personal friend, Sadhu Parimal Bandhu, who, as a Holy Man of India, was much loved by these natives. In sympathy with our long search, and possibly some private esoteric interests of his own, he had brought us to this legendary place—the fabled room where, it is said, the Sage Jagadbandhu spent fifteen years of his life shut away in hermitage from the world in consecrated meditation.

Ron was going to enter that "Hindu Holy of Holies," as I elect to call it, on this special night and spend, if possible, a number of hours within the sacred room. I qualify our (or rather Ron's) intention with the "if possible," as rumor had it that no man could stand the room's tumultuous psychic forces.

"A half-hour in the room and they come out like babbling fools," Sadhu Parimal Bandhu had said.

India had proved a strange and colorful country with fabulous temples, magnificent mosques, and exotic bazaars; a veritable fairyland of the unusual that kept us busily taking pictures.

Ron and I had divided our work. Mine was the job of gathering and recording data, while he probed with his cameras and searched out East Indian lore with the yearning of a hungry soul. Ron had a special desire to do some shooting around the outcast area of the Doms. Everyone seemed adamantly opposed to this suggestion, but being of the tenacious temperament of a motion-picture man geared to get what he wanted when he wanted it, it didn't surprise me too much when he announced that that was precisely what he was going to do. I had half expected that, but when he announced that he intended entering the untenantable Sacred Room of Jagadbandhu in the same area, it was almost too much. For even though he was spiritually inclined, the Doms have never been too friendly with occidentals. But win, lose, or draw, we were in this together, and if Ron did enter the room, I knew that I would not be far away. Also I knew that Sadhu had instigated the idea and would be nearby.

The clatter of a cymbal-beat close to my ear snapped me back to the immediate reality. It was picked up by a clanking bell rung in the hands of a half-naked boy. Another cymbal from another part of the crowd added its brassy clang, and yet another, and another. Then a voice was raised in song, and soon all else was forgotten in the din of the natives' *kirtan* as the religious song-fest of the Hindus became a bedlam!

As I mentioned previously, Provoo Jagadbandhu is the counterpart of Jesus Christ to the Christian, the Buddha to the Buddhists, and Mohammed to the Mohammedans. He is the Hindu's Messiah. Dead some fifty years, his picture is to be seen in many *ashrams* and countless homes in West Bengal and Eastern Pakistan, where it is worshipped.

To his devotees, Jagadbandhu is regarded as the Savior of the Hindus, and his body is preserved in a secret place in Northern India, awaiting its physical resurrection. As with the Christ and His second coming, "No man shall know the day nor the hour," but it is prophesied that Jagadbandhu will appear again in the flesh, and

Crowds of Hindus continually stream before the shrine of Provoo Jagadbandhu, messiah of the "untouchables."

Enshrined picture of the Provoo Jagadbandhu, messiah of the Doms, Calcutta, India.

his coming will usher in a great spiritual revolution in India.

Like the Buddha, Provoo Jagadbandhu lived the most humble of lives, and his reported miracles were such as to gather a great following about him; followers who, on his death, raised him to the status of sainthood—Jagadbandhu, Messiah of the Untouchables.

To repeat briefly his history, as a sage living among men, Jagadbandhu developed the most remarkable of spiritual powers, and retreated into a small room in Calcutta in the midst of the poverty-ridden quarters of his beloved Doms, in which he remained for fifteen years of his life. His daily needs were tended to through a small doorway by his followers, and it is said that during those fifteen long years of voluntary seclusion he became more than man; he gained the power to send his spirit soaring on astral flights to confer with other advanced souls and became one with God.

I felt a nudge on my elbow; it was Ron Ormond and he was nodding toward the Sadhu. I looked among the swirling mass of

Throngs of Hindus gather before the sacred room of Jagadbandhu to witness the American's admittance.

Ron Ormond entering the sacred room of Provoo Jagadbandhu.

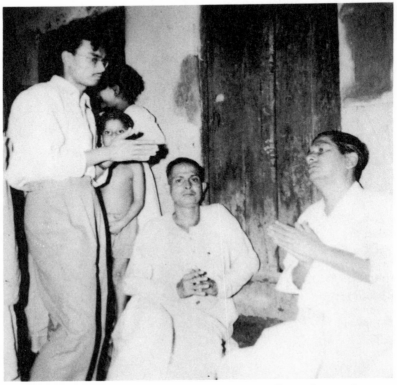

The door is closed and the long vigil for Ron Ormond commences in darkness.

Three hours and thirty-five minutes later the door opens.

bodies and saw the Holy Man beckoning my partner into the Sacred Room of Jagadbandhu. By now the jingling of cymbals amid the sharp percussion of drums increased to a maddening crescendo. A robe, one that Jagadbandhu had personally worn, was placed about Ron's shoulders. The din of the *kirtan* was deafening. Sadhu Parimal Bandhu took a firm grip on Ron's arm and started leading him toward the room. Ron glanced back momentarily and said something, but I could not catch the words over the noise of the crowd. Moments later he was seated cross-legged on the floor in the dingy little room. Sadhu walked out solemnly as I watched expectantly, as though waiting for Jagadbandhu to appear, right on the spot, that very moment. He closed the door behind him; there was but scant light in the street in the gloomy depths between the buildings, and with the door closed the interior of the room was undoubtedly plunged into darkness. Ron Ormond was alone.

I have mentioned how magically a crowd can gather in India.

What had happened before was as nothing, for now the hundred persons had multiplied at least five times. The place took on the atmosphere of a gigantic rally; people were running in from every direction.

Suddenly there was a great commotion, unlike anything I had heard before. I quickly looked toward the door to see if everything was alright. Then I discovered the cause of the commotion to be a white sacred cow, its horns painted a violent red, ankling along the narrow street. Even though the street was full to the point of bulging, the crowd gave and made a slender pathway for the animal. All eyes seemed to be focused on the beast as though it were some sort of omen. Slowly the cow approached the room, then, stepping toward the doorway, lowered its head. Probably to sniff at one of the discarded flower garlands, I thought. But it seems that I was

When the door opens, Ron Ormond arises from his meditation and leaves the sacred room. Eager hands seek prashade *from him.*

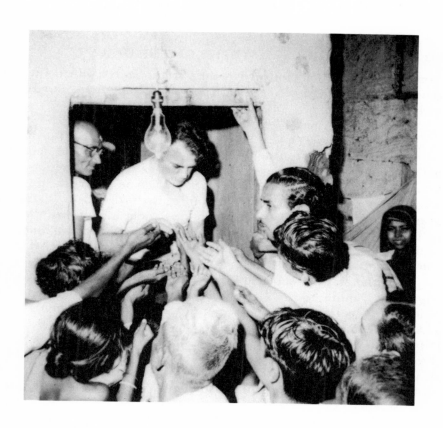

alone in that opinion, for, above the *kirtan,* Sadhu yelled, "It is a good omen, he bowed his head in front of the room and your friend within."

"What does it mean?" I yelled back.

"The Provoo will appear to your friend," responded Parimal.

Just as lazily as it had walked in, the animal walked out. By now the *kirtan* had reached an even wilder pinnacle of volume and frenzy. From the glassy look in the eyes of some it struck me that a sort of hypnotic hysteria was beginning to take place. I glanced at my watch; my partner had been in that room almost the allotted half-hour. I wondered what was going through his mind and whether he had encountered the great psychic force of the presence of Jagadbandhu that Sadhu had predicted?

Then the watch's hands told me the half-hour was up. Would Ron come running out a babbling idiot? The crowd seemed to be measuring the time with the same expectancy, for somehow now, and despite the *kirtan,* everything seemed strangely quiet. But the critical half-hour passed and became an hour, then two, and then three. By now the crowd had swelled into several thousand yelling Bengalis, pushing and shoving into the alleys of the area. Many of them were devout followers of Jagadbandhu; many were simply curiosity-seekers.

I looked around for Sadhu Parimal, who must have sensed this, because moments afterward he appeared at my side.

"Your partner has done a remarkable thing," he said. "No one has been able to withstand the room's forces before."

I became apprehensive. Perhaps something had happened to Ron. My anxiety must have shown on my face, for Sadhu said, "He will be out soon."

"Good," was all I could answer.

Exactly three hours and thirty-five minutes after Ron Ormond entered the room, the door opened, seemingly of its own volition, as if by some magical means. I looked in and tried to make my way to the door, but it was impossible. Hundreds of Bengalis were already ahead of me and crowding the entrance. I tried for a vantage spot and made it up to a nearby step. My partner rose unsteadily to his feet. Parimal Bandhu forced his way through the crowd and handed Ron some *prashade.* Ormond opened his mouth and took the religious food solemnly. Then, as is the custom, he took a piece of the sacred food and gingerly put it into the mouth of the Sadhu. Instantly a score of eager hands were held out in appeal for some of the same.

By now the Hindus were whipped into a religious frenzy, many yelling, *"Hari, hari, hari!"* My eyes dilated as I continued to watch, and one of the Hindus kneeled to Ron's feet and kissed them.

Others began doing the same thing in a long advancing line, while still others came on to simply reach down to touch the American's foot with their hand, and then placed their fingers reverently to their forehead.

It was quite a ceremony, and I could see that Ron was considerably embarrassed. A thought flashed through my mind. He had entered the mysterious room a perfectly normal American adventurer; he now had seemingly turned into a kind of saint in the Hindus' eyes. Maybe Jagadbandhu had, indeed, placed favor on him.

For approximately two hours the Doms pressed close around my partner. Standing always next to him was Parimal Bandhu, as hundreds of Hindus struggled to touch his feet. As for me, I could only observe, not daring to get too close to my adventurous friend, for by now, even though the *kirtan* had stopped, the Doms yelled and shouted so loudly it was impossible to speak. Furthermore, Hindus can be excitable, and I did not want to run the risk of trying to remove Ron from his now-fervent devotees, lest I start a major conflict.

A couple of hours later I squeezed Ron into a small taxi and we headed back toward our hotel. I had a million questions to ask, but in particular I would settle for one answer—did Provoo Jagadbandhu really manifest himself? When I asked, he simply smiled.

"Well," I pressed, "don't hold an old pal in suspense. Did he?"

"I think he did, Mac, I think he did," Ron answered.

"What do you mean, you think he did? Don't you know?"

Ron looked thoughtful for a moment, then replied, "Well, there is sometimes a very thin dividing-line between what is conscious and what is subconscious. By the same token, there is likewise the same thin dividing-line between reality and spirituality."

He settled back deep into the seat of the taxi as it rattled along, and continued, "I resolved patiently to see it through; I admit, I put some stock in that rumor about the power of the room, but I also had my doubts."

I looked at my friend, hardly able to contain myself as I waited for him to continue.

"Sitting on a stone floor isn't so bad at first, but try it for an hour. Before long the cramps that develop in your muscles become sheer agony. But then, that was the turning point," he finished.

"The turning point? What do you mean?" I asked.

"As you know, I learned a process of Buddhistic meditation in Thailand called Vipassana. Within the room of Jagadbandhu I decided to try it. It had helped me during that "buried-alive" experience, you will recall. This time I figured it would help me pass the time and take my mind off my cramped muscles."

Ron's mention of Vipassana reminded me of the time he had

The veneration of Ron Ormond by the Hindus, following his three hour and thirty-five minute sojourn within the sacred room of Provoo Jagadbandhu.

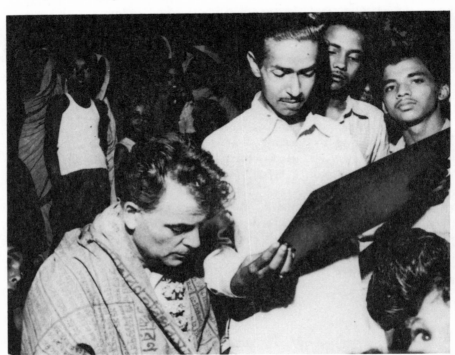

spent at Wat Pak Nam, in Bangkok, in pursuit of that unique method of "going within." "What about the cramps in your muscles?" I asked. "Did they subside?"

"At first it was rather difficult, but gradually I focused my mind on the din of the *kirtan* outside and before long a numbness came over my legs and the pain melted away."

"You mean the *kirtan* rhythms lulled you into this mental anesthetic and took away the pain?"

"That's one of the things I meant when I mentioned a thin dividing-line between the conscious and the subconscious; all I know is that the pain went away and yet I was still conscious. That is, I think I was conscious," he corrected.

I thought of what Parimal Bandhu, the holy man, had told us —that rhythmic sound is an important instrument to the completion of "going within" by the Hindu method. Perhaps that explained why so many holy men in the Orient chanted their prayers. In India, the sacred sound OM (AUM) represents the whole phenomena of sound producing and is considered the matrix of all the variety of possible sounds. I mentioned this in the chapter dealing with the art of meditation. As I recalled in the *kirtan,* the OM sound was certainly a definite part of it, and was positively hypnotic in its effect. I listened, appraising every word.

"I was fully awake and mentally alert," Ron continued, "and although my eyes were closed, a subdued glow penetrated beneath my lids, as though the room had suddenly become lighted."

"That's impossible," I informed him. "There was no way for a light to get into the room."

"That's what I mean," Ron finished. "I thought so, too, and opened my eyes to see if someone had entered the room with me. No one had, as you know, but to me it seemed as though the room was lit up like a Christmas tree."

"Fantastic!" I breathed, waiting for him to continue.

"I had the feeling of another presence in the room, but I must confess I saw no one—just the radiant glow—then I uttered one word."

I waited anxiously for him to go on.

"My throat was tense, but I nevertheless heard myself saying, 'Jagadbandhu!' "

"What made you say that?"

"I don't know, Mac, I just don't know. . . ." He paused for a moment, then: "But I do know that it was one of the most wonderful experiences I have ever had. Now, I've a question to ask you."

"Go ahead."

"How long was I in that room?"

"Three hours and thirty-five minutes," I furnished. "Why?"

"I had no idea that I was in there for more than twenty or twenty-five minutes."

I looked speculatively at my companion as the taxi whizzed us along the Calcutta streets.

"Do you mind if I go back to a question about the Provoo?"

"I imagine you want to know more about the sacred room," he replied.

"Precisely," I came back. "I want you to recall, to the best of your knowledge, the details of the room when it was lighted."

"Okay."

"Was it anything like Joseph Smith of the Mormon's vision about the *personage* standing before him in a glowing white robe?"

"It wasn't that way at all," Ron stated. "There was no personage, and while there was a glow that was visible to my eyes, it was also a glow that I seemed to feel inside of my very being."

"Then it was nothing like the reports of materialization in seances that we sometimes hear about in the States?"

"Nothing like that at all, Mac. It was like some latent power that had been lying dormant had been suddenly awakened and gave you a power to feel or contact the spiritual. We've been studying oriental religions and methods of meditation for some time now, but the mind all too frequently has certain handicaps and lacks the necessary ability to concentrate fully, properly; perhaps it's because of the multiplicity of daily trials one has to meet. Parimal Bandhu told me of the need to go beyond the sense-world and enter the region of inner-reality. Some call it 'cosmic consciousness,' I believe."

I knew what Ron referred to. The idea has been advanced that there are three forms of consciousness: simple consciousness, found in the lower animals; self-consciousness, found in normal man; and cosmic consciousness, an evolutionary form of consciousness toward which man was progressing, and which some specially favored individuals had testified to experiencing. It is described as a phenomenon of mental illumination accompanied by the physical experience of perceiving a bright light.

Ron continued, "It was a wonderful experience. I cannot describe it better than to say it was *soul satisfying*. Perhaps it was the Provoo who helped me find it, I honestly don't know, but I do know that it was something in or of that room that made it possible."

Ron talked very little after that statement; although he seemed exhilarated, he also showed signs of fatigue. After all, almost seven hours had been devoted to the experience; the time spent in meditation, the hours afterward, when the Doms refused to allow us to leave, plus the drive to and from the location. Even so, we were both most pleased with the success of the day.

We can theorize about it, of course, along the lines that objects absorb some of the life-force of the living, and later reflect it back to a sensitive person. This process is called psychometry. It could have been something like that, or maybe it was simply the result of an overworking imagination under the stimulus of the exciting *kirtan* and the emotion of the situation. Or perhaps it was truly a manifestation of the returned presence of Jagadbandhu within those sacred walls, precisely as Parimal Bandhu said it would occur.

We would like to go back someday and investigate further. But the fact remains that we entered a forbidden area amid the most obvious scowls of disapproval, and before the end of the day I saw my partner leave that same area the object of sincere veneration in the eyes of a race not normally very approving of people of our color.

Something assuredly had happened that drastically changed the attitude of a multitude, and brought us closer to understanding the great religious mysteries of the Orient.

The world-famous Temple of Jainism, Calcutta, India.

19

Conclusions of the Journey

I have seen many lands, witnessed strange happenings, participated in unusual forms of worship, and spoken with astute minds of the East. My journey with my partner, Ron Ormond (including Ron's illumination and our long discussions of these subjects) in the search for great religious mysteries of the Orient has brought me answers to questions I have long sought.

We, of the western nations, have greatly developed the technical aspects of our lives. Eastern people, on the other hand, have greatly developed the spiritual. Indeed, the spiritual is part and parcel of their daily living, just as the scientific is implicit in ours. In the Orient, much is subjective and personal, while, in the West, we have the advantage of being objective, and thus, have greater opportunities to expand our horizons. Hence, I am able to present a composite of eastern religious knowledge with sweeping scope, giving the oriental answers to questions asked by every man. I regard these as the "conclusions of the journey."

Consider these answers as you will, but rest assured that there are no snap judgements here. These answers are the result of ages of meditation and deep thought on the part of sages, and are the culmination of opinions and convictions from various cultures throughout the Far East as to the truth about ourselves, our inner nature, and our spiritual heritage of immortality.

Ron and I have found these thoughts that our journey into the unknown brought to us both interesting and helpful; we accordingly pass them along to others.

So, as much as is possible, let me personally step aside and simply lay before the reader these insights as they are proclaimed by millions in the Orient. How truthful these conclusions are we will all eventually know.

ON THE QUESTION OF GOD.

God is held as being omnipotent, omnipresent, and omniscient. Thus, he is *all,* ever-present, with infinite knowledge and power. As such, God is correctly named (in whatever religion, belief, or conception) "The Almighty!"

In one school of thought, He is seen as an omnipotent *personal* being, while, at the opposite extreme, others regard "God" as an *impersonal* universal force. Between these two extremes come the many variations of man's conception of God. But, universal to all beliefs, whatever is called or named as God is invariably regarded as possessing the quality of omnipotence. There is the answer. For, if God is omnipotent, He is all-inclusive, and, as such, can be both a personal being and a universal force, and encompass every possible aspect of man's conception of Him.

In different countries, to different races, God is known by a variety of names. But such names actually have no meaning other than in the understanding and the personalizing of their conception of God by a name having meaning to each particular group of people.

It has often been quoted that "God created man in his own image." This provides the opportunity for insight into the nature of God; the greater man understands himself, the greater will be his understanding of God. For God, as an omnipotent being, is both within and without of you. And you are one with God, for if man is created in the image of God and man has the uniqueness of independent being and self-consciousness, then it follows that God, likewise, has these qualities. And yet God is also an impersonal force in nature, viz., as an omnipotent being, God has all qualities; He is The Almighty, the Center of All.

ON THE QUESTION OF RELIGION.

Closely related to the question of God lies the question of religion, which presents a way of worship of God. As we all know, there are many variations in such practices.

Some people seem to find religious satisfaction in one creed and some in others. The conclusion seems to be that the religion a person or group of people gravitate toward depends much upon the psychological makeup of the individuals involved. For example, for western understanding, considering the matter within the structure of Christianity only, some find in the ceremonial nature of Catholicism the manner of worship they like. Others, with possibly more democratic tastes, prefer Protestantism. Those who hold to a sort of self-realization lean toward Christian Science and the "God Within" type of churches, while those with esoteric interests find Religious Science, metaphysics, and various cult-like religions greatly appealing.

And in the broad, world-wide sense of nations and cultures, whole races of people tend toward certain variations in religious practice, such as Christianity generally among Nordic people, the Moslem faith among the Arab nations, and Hinduism, Buddhism, etc. among the people of the Orient.

And each names God by a different name and worships Him in a great diversity of practices. Such diversity of religious beliefs and practices has been the despair of many seeking to find religion, for it so often seems that if even religions and/or religious people can't find harmony among themselves, then it is a field one would do well to depart from.

But God is omnipotent, so, as the Almighty, all names, practices, and beliefs apply to Him, no matter what they may be. Since God is omnipotent, no religion is wrong; the understanding must be that religion should be regarded as a designed means of worshipping God; religion is a way of expressing one's self in appreciation of God and, in a preferred manner, to reach out toward that which is Omnipotent.

This is the answer to harmony in the ever-present disharmony that many divergent religions seem to have produced. Appreciate that all people are different and each finds his own way (both as an individual and as a special group) that brings him the unique satisfaction that his special selection of a religion provides.

And is worship pleasing to God? Of course. Man is created in God's image. Worship brings satisfaction to man; thus, it does likewise to God, viz.: religion in definition is man's method (in whatever variety this may entail) of reaching (worshiping) that which is regarded as omnipotent in the hope (belief) that he will, himself, become a part of and/or partake of that omnipotence. The diversity of religions are but an illusion, for in reality man is part and parcel of that very omnipotence which he seeks. The oriental religions especially appreciate this truth. Thus, no matter in what or which manner man reaches for God it is impossible for him not to find God, *all religions being simply diverse roads that lead to the same place (the God source)*.

ON THE QUESTION OF MAN.

Man is a trinity of body, soul, and spirit. The body is the physical mechanism in which man is manifested. The soul is the real man (the person, the ego, the specific individual self). The spirit is man's divinity, his direct linkage with the oneness of God. It is the link with God and/or the God-source; it is the God Within and the God Without; it is the Universal Force in nature; it is *all*. Here are more specific details of this consideration, viz.:

THE BODY. This is entirely a physical machine that is occupied by the soul during a specific period of inhabitance for the specific purpose of the evolution of the self (soul). In due time, that "machine" will wear out and must be discarded, to which process the term, "death" is applied. It is a term of much psychological disturbance to many people, for it seems to so finalize and bring to a termination the individual. Especially in the Occident, death is met with lamentation. In the Orient, it is much better understood, and in some cases is even met with joy, as though "the passing on" of the individual has concluded a chapter of tribulation.

Actually, the process of death should be no more feared than removing one suit of clothes and putting on another, for the process no more marks the termination of a man as an individual than does the junking of his automobile after it has seen better days and has eventually worn out its usefulness. The man simply goes on to seek a new car. More will be said on the question of death in another section.

But the body is not the originator of its own performance; such is the function of the soul.

The human brain is the ultimate product of physical evolution. It has amazing capacities and functions more remarkable than the most complicated computer. Indeed, the brain may be likened to a computer; it performs what it is programmed to perform. Exactly like the computer, it operates entirely as it is directed by the operator behind it. For the brain, itself, is not self-operating. On conception, the soul enters the body and begins to assume occupancy of the driver's seat (brain), as the control center of the body.

If the brain is in perfect shape it performs its specific function well; if impaired, then it performs in a faulty manner.

Examples of this observation are obvious in such cases as brain damage at birth. Such a person frequently goes through life without ever functioning efficiently. There is nothing wrong with the driver (soul) behind it, but the machine is damaged so it does not perform as it should. And the same applies not only to the brain, but to all portions of the body. If the machinery can be repaired so as to function properly then the soul will be able to operate the body smoothly, as it should. If the damage, however, cannot be or is not repaired, then the soul must function as best it can in the damaged mechanism it occupies for this incarnation. Such an instance isn't as disheartening as it might seem at first, for the purpose of the soul-in-body experience is for the purpose of *soul evolution,* and experience, even in an impaired or imperfect body, is still experience which sums up to the ultimate development of the soul.

All knowledge that is developed through the soul's skillful use of the brain instrument becomes the eternal property of the soul, as part of the product of its evolution.

Remember the foregoing truth. How fortunate this is, for how frequently we hear of a brain packed with years of brilliance suddenly becoming childlike in performance from the mere action of a clot of blood blocking off its food supply. Or through advancing senility, as old age creeps on, lessening the blood flow, causing its performance to decline drastically.

It is difficult for the individual to think of himself as a personality independent of the body he inhabits. The reasons lie in the fact that, as the embryo develops, is born, and grows into maturity, the soul becomes more and more fused within the body and a unity develops between the two and it becomes difficult to conceive of one without the other. Also, there is an amnesia-effect on soul-body entry causing the "sense of continuity" to be temporarily discontinued during the body's habitation that further intensifies the illusion of oneness and onlyness.

Is it possible for the soul to leave the body and is it possible for the soul to regain remembrances of its previous experiences (incarnations) while still living in the body? Yes, to both questions. The oriental masters can do this, but rarely has western man obtained the skill. So, unless one seeks to especially develop these unique talents, it must be said, generally speaking, that it is only at death that the soul may slip free from the intertwining effects of its physical habitation. At that time, the process becomes spontaneous and is actually automatic in nature as the physical ties of the "vital life force" drop away.

THE SOUL. Look into a mirror and study your eyes. You will see your real self looking out from within as though through the glass of a window. How remarkably penetrating is the simple phrase, "The eyes are the windows to the soul."

Your real self is the soul. This is the specific individual that is "you"; this is the "driver" that sits within the control-center of the brain and operates the body you inhabit.

And there is only one of you in the entire universe. Absolutely nowhere is there another exactly to match yourself; you are an individual, a specific ego, a certain self, and you will, thus, ever and always be you. For the soul (through its spiritual tie with God) is immortal, and, both as an individual entity and, also, in relation to its oneness with God, is everlasting.

THE SPIRIT. Man is created in God's own image. God is within man. Oneness with the God-source. All of these are but different ways of expressing the role of the spirit. The spirit is man's divine linkage with God. It is man's divinity. It is man's immortality. It is man's heritage. It is the purpose of his entire evolvement—physically, mentally, and spiritually.

Such is the uniqueness of man. Man, accordingly, is seen as a soul in body incarnate, in direct linkage with God.

ON THE QUESTION OF LIFE.

Life is a vital force produced by a combination of physical and spiritual factors. It is a gift from God, and pervades the universe. It is in all matter, but is not sparked into action until it combines with the organic. As a symbolic illustration, in relation to man, regard life as the fuel that feeds the lamp of the body. In the beginning of a new life the flame burns feebly; gradually, with the coming of maturity—in the prime of life—the flame reaches its zenith; then, as the years pass on into old age the flame burns less and less brightly until it is eventually extinguished with the advent of death.

It is not that the vital fuel is ever diminished; its supply is inexhaustible, but entirely that the instrument through which it functions varies in its efficiency to burn it.

A tragedy?

One can hardly expect a lamp to burn forever. Also, there are many new lamps to be lighted. Just bear in mind that while the body is mortal and to dust returneth, the soul (the real "you" as a unique individual) is everlasting and is immortal. It is the thought of death bringing with it the cessation of the immediate life and the dissolution of the body that one has come to know so intimately and fondly (as one's current body-home) that is disturbing. Death seems so much like a permanent closing of the door. Such feelings are certainly understandable, just as it would be a shock if one's house were suddenly destroyed in a cataclysm. Yet there are countless new homes to lease.

ON THE QUESTION OF DEATH.

Rather than looking upon death as the "closing of the door," in the Orient it is looked upon as the *opening of the door,* the passing onward to further adventures in living, for the life of man is immortal. What is much of the fear of death is really a fear of the unknown, and yet, death is not nearly so unknown to us as most people seem to feel. For we have a pattern before us constantly of both death and of our living in the afterlife.

We die in a sense every night, to arise next morning to pick up the active threads of existence and continue on. The experience of sleep and the experience of death are counterparts in relation to what we will personally experience.

And what is the pattern for life in the hereafter? It is the world of dreams with which everyone is familiar. A dream to the dreamer, at the time of its experience, has every bit as much reality as does physical existence, yet it is not bounded within the limitation of the physical body; it enjoys the unbounded freedom of the mind. The soul, in its realm, enjoys exactly the same parallel of freedom and experience as does the dreamer in his dreams.

These patterns for both an understanding of death and the afterlife have been provided us in the infinite wisdom of God, that man through understanding may lose entirely his fear of the unknown.

There are four very pertinent questions relative to this subject that have been asked countless times: Does the soul feel pain? Is death a painful experience when the soul leaves the body? Does the soul have life everlasting? What is reincarnation?

These answers are from the sages. They are expounded here, one by one.

1. Yes, the soul does feel pain; in fact, it participates intimately in every sensation and experience of the body it inhabits. Who should know this better than you, as you, personally, experience pain in all manner of forms, both physically and mentally. And well it is, for such experiences constitute much of your purpose in this body's habitation.

2. No, death is not a painful experience, and the soul's leaving of the body, with the coming of death, holds no more remembered sensation of its exit than it does of its entry. While the soul may experience pain all through its in-body term, with the coming of death all pain ceases.

As I have mentioned, entering the state of death, in regard to sensation, is exactly analogous to entering the state of sleep. Indeed, during deep sleep the soul is partially "out of body" (out of phase with body, as it were) —a state surprisingly close to death. The sages of the East call it "the little death."

3. Does the soul have life everlasting? One may answer "no" or "yes" to that question depending upon what one regards as "life." Physical life is definitely not everlasting, it is mortal, and when its burning of the vital force of life snuffs out, that particular organism that was vitalized ceases to be (dies). However, life can also be used as a term meaning continuation of self-consciousness, indentity, the living on of the ego (call it as one wishes: self, mind, or soul); this is immortal and as such is everlasting.

4. Reincarnation. Oriental thought has more penetrated this subject than has the Occident. Reincarnation is simply the term desig-

nating the evolution of the soul. Experience after experience must be engaged in by the soul—in numerous body habitations—to achieve the culmination of its growth. This subject will be discussed further in the next section.

ON THE QUESTION OF EVOLUTION.

Evolution is the evolvement of the body. Reincarnation is the evolvement of the soul.

Evolution is the way of growth in nature. All things must evolve and change. Nothing can ever merely stand still. The term "evolution," as we commonly use it, applies to that which is of the physical. It has meaning in the gradual development of physical life-forms ever changing.

The term "reincarnation" applies to that which is of the soul. As does the body, the soul evolves, and, in direct relationship to it, so does the spirit.

Through the life-experiences in physical bodies lies the way for the evolution of the soul as it grows and expands. Body after body, or, more correctly expressed, life-experience after life-experience must be manifested. Eventually the growth of each self is such that the use of further bodies for development will not be needed as the soul reaches (as the Hindus well express it) the state of nirvana, or oneness with God, as its ultimate goal.

And yet in oneness with God there is ever individuality for there is but the one of you and thus ever will be, and yet the higher your evolvement the more in oneness you become. A paradox? Not at all, for you are created in God's image and hence partake of the aspects of God, and all is complete in omnipotence.

ON THE QUESTION OF THE REALM OF THE SOUL.

Eastern adepts invite you to take a step with them into the beyond.

The realm of the soul is the realm of "mind." It is a realm governed by laws of its own completely divergent from those of the physical world that we know so personally. And yet, out-of-body, the soul retains a continuity of memory and identity with all of its experiences—in repeated existences—in the physical world. And, as it evolutionizes, it advances ever-upward toward oneness with God, and the continuing expansion of its God-consciousness.

Western people today appreciate that there are so-called "powers of mind," being studied in parapsychology, referred to as Extra Sensory Perception (ESP) and the Psi Powers, that belong to the realm of the soul. Such phenomena as telepathy, telekinesis, teleportation, etc., are of obvious paramount value to out-of-body experience. These abilities are the means of communication, movement, and manifestation of the soul when in its own realm, and while "in body" they may be cultivated and utilized to an extent, out-of-body they are readily applicable.

In mind, the soul lives in a realm of dreams, dreams made up of its collection of experiences from repeated incarnations. The greater its development, the greater the scope of its dreams. And what dreams! Dreams in the soul-realm are the dreams of a free mind that are as real to that mind as any possible physical reality. The mind has no limit in its scope other than that imposed by its own state of evolution. It can soar to the heights or plunge to the depths. It can reach the stars, live in golden mansions, love, achieve, create, do whatever it desires. Here in the soul-realm is found the "heaven" of all religions, eastern or western.

And what of "Hell?" It is the grosser "below"—the physical existence to which each soul must return until its evolution is complete and no further incarnations are needed, and the heaven state becomes eternal. To burn in fire in hell is merely symbolism for the tortures of the physical state that each soul must endure. The "hellfires" that burn forever yet do not destroy temper the steel of the individual being in the forge of the physical existences through which each soul must pass in its development. How many incarnations (hells) each soul must go through depends entirely upon the life one lives in each incarnation. Some achieve the heaven state (oneness with God) in shorter spans, others in longer.[1]

These are all innate concepts of eastern religions. Does the soul possess a body in the mind state? The oriental masters say that "free mind" does not actually need a body, but that it is capable of enveloping itself in a body—in the astral sense of a body—of the most tenuous nature. The continual usage of physical bodies has placed a sort of "body-awareness" upon the individual as a mark of individual identification in both the mind and the physical realms.

The soul, in its own realm, is no stranger to sleep; long periods of its out-of-body experiences are spent in such a related condition, for regeneration and strengthening.

Eventually a call comes upon each individual soul that has as yet not completed its cycles of development, and the time for leaving

---

1. Observe the close alliance of this realm, inhabited by the soul following death, to that entered by the individual in meditation. They are the same, for meditation points the way toward the realm of the soul. But, blissful as it is, in-body soul experience is but a small fraction of the out-of-body soul experience. However, the glory is still sufficient for the sage to observe, "Meditation makes possible the entering of the 'Kingdom of Heaven' while still living in the human body."

its native realm of mind becomes urgent and it must again enter body and assume the physical. Each incarnation will differ, depending upon the specific needs of each individual soul. Some will incarnate in male gender, others in female. Some incarnations will be for sizable periods, others for short; some will bring much development, others very little.

How long will the process of reincarnation continue? As the sages comment, it varies with each individual soul. It will continue for as long as it is needed for that individual soul to reach that stage in its evolution where reincarnations in the physical are no longer necessary. The time is long, but it is not infinite, and ultimately each soul will find *nirvana* (oneness with God).

ON THE QUESTION OF LIFE AFTER DEATH.

Let it be asked again, do we live after we die? Of course, for it is quite impossible to kill a man. The body, as a physical mechanism, can be destroyed, in which event its occupancy by the soul must be abandoned; but this is no more death, in the sense of non-continuation of existence, than is leaving an old house and preparing to move into a new one.

Were this not so, life would be a great travesty and the ultimate of tragedies. For, from the physical standpoint, all goes downhill. We commence in the body as an infant that gradually matures to reach its peak of perfection in function, and then, assuredly, starts on the decline to eventual complete uselessness. Occurring naturally, we call it "old age," in which the body-machine simply wears out and no longer performs as it should. And the soul, thus, can no longer function well through it. Occurring as the result of an accident, disease, or other cause prior to the wearing-out process of aging, such merely brings about the termination of the body's usefulness that much sooner.

In such events, death occurs, at which time the soul can leave the now-to-be-discarded mechanism of the used-up body. Death is only an illusion of tragedy. Man is immortal and simply proceeds onward from one body to the next during the process of the soul's evolution. There is a programming in the soul, in each incarnation, that produces an amnesia effect which blocks out the memory experiences from one physical life to the next while each body is occupied (in some rare instances, this blockage can be looked beyond), but, as a free soul, the memory and individual identity is maintained as an intimate part of the process.

ON THE QUESTION OF ULTIMATE JUSTICE.

As a supplement to the above section, how often are ideas like these expressed:

Unless we die prematurely through disease or accident, we live but to end our lives in dissolution as the years advance, senility sets in upon us, and all goes downward to the grave.

The world is filled with evil and more often than not that which is evil prospers while that which is good fails. There is no justice.

The world is a battleground of wars, heartbreak, and sorrow. Happiness is far outweighed by sadness.

All such thoughts are true, as every man is only too well aware. And yet there is ultimate justice. For it is not the purpose of this world to be a haven of utopia; it is a battleground of experience. Evil predominates on earth and far exceeds that which is good, all of which makes what good is achieved the more meaningful. There is a purpose in it all, and that purpose is to bring experience to the soul.

A soul must return for repeated experiences in this battleground of tribulation, over and over and over, until it reaches a stage in its development when such experience is no longer needed. Oriental belief is purposely repetitious on these points, and such is the way they were presented to us in every country we explored. With repetition comes understanding. The adepts say that these concepts cannot possibly be overemphasized if their full comprehension is to be mastered. Incarnations are experiences "in hell," in which the soul is gradually burnished in the "fire" to become a thing of beauty. Its ultimate purpose is toward oneness with God, which is of the good. Hence, if the soul lives toward such purpose, it evolves that much faster and completes its incarnations. Conversely, a life wasted in evil not only accomplishes little in relation to its development, but may actually retard its growth, thus prolonging its "in-hell" periods (separation from its own heaven-realm and from God) in difficult physical existences.

Reincarnation is the only concept that holds within it ultimate justice. The wealth of understanding it brings is in the growth of good within the soul that leads it eventually to oneness with God.

ON THE QUESTION OF CHRISTIANITY.

As I was gaining knowledge for a western audience, I was especially anxious to get the slants from great students of eastern religions in relation to the subject of Christianity. I wanted their personal viewpoint. I asked some point-blank questions and received some point-blank answers.

First and foremost, eastern sages have a very sincere and deep respect for the religion of Christianity; they regard it as one of the great religions of the world. Likewise, they hold the Master Jesus in high esteem (they even claim some records affirming that Jesus made a pilgrimage to India during the secret years of his absence from the Holy Land). They present the following observations:

CHRISTIANITY. As a religion it is a special system for the worshiping of God that is better adapted for occidental nations than oriental.

THE BIBLE. Every religion has its sacred writings; for Christianity this means of course, the Holy Bible. Two questions are frequently asked about this remarkable book, i.e., is the Bible the inspired word of God, and, if so, why do there appear to be so many seemingly contradictory elements in it? And the answers to the questions? Most assuredly The Bible is the inspired word of God, but it must not be regarded as a book merely to be read from cover to cover, word for word, as a story or record. Rather, it must be regarded as a book containing the great truths, but truths cloaked in symbolism, symbolism that must be probed and searched out to bring forth the true meanings. The book is replete with flashes of cosmic consciousness that give insight into the nature and manner of God. As for having contradictory elements, as has been stated, the Bible is the inspired word of God; it has not been stated that it was written by God. The Bible, as a book, was written by men incarnate in the flesh and is subject to all the failings that belong to the flesh. Years of separation by different writers, miles of separation in different localities, and translation after translation have all taken their toll. The smooth writing of any book is to be expected only when it is the work of an individual, or occasionally that of a closely-knit team working on a mutual project. The Bible is anything but that. It is truly amazing that it is at all unified. Also, it must be borne in mind that it is more than just the word of God, it is also the history of particular peoples during particular times, a collection of codes and ancient laws, etc. relative to the times of its writing.

But the insights of God are there, and may be discovered by all who seek. But remember, in reading it that much of what is expressed is written in symbols and examples. To illustrate this point, consider some aspects important to the religion of Christianity.

GOD AND THE DEVIL. All that *is* follows the ruling of both positive and negative aspects. God is the *positive,* referred to as "good," while the Devil (Satan), is the *negative,* referred to as "evil." Even in the realm of the soul, which the Christian terms Heaven, we have this element of conflict between the two.

The realm of the soul (which we can also call the Realm of God, if we so elect), is a separate creation from that of the physical realm, and is the habitation of souls; souls of high evolvement being continuous to the realm, while souls in evolution must enter the realm of the physical until such perfect evolvement is achieved.

The Biblical term applied to souls in the God-realm is angels, of which Satan was one of the highest until (as the Bible story relates), after a challenge of God's supremacy, he was cast down into Hell (earth). (We point instinctively upward when thinking of Heaven and downward [earthward] when thinking of Hell.)

"And Satan was given dominion over the Earth." Even in this there is purpose, since there must always be conflict if there is to be growth, and in the domination of Satan on earth is provided the very finest of arenas for the development of souls through the mastering of the stresses imposed by evil. With "the forces of evil," ascendant on earth, it is little wonder that they predominate here, and so many sadnesses and seeming injustices are apparent. However, conversely, it is through the continuous conflicts with evil that good becomes very *good* indeed.

In Christianity, it is common to look upon God as a personal being. Is the Devil, also, to be so regarded? Of course, for in omnipotence both the personal and impersonal are ever-present, and to deny Satan lack of individuality is to make him less than oneself, which obviously is not the case.

THE TRINITY. God is referred to, in the Bible, as being the Father, the Son, and the Holy Ghost. There is excellent symbolism in God being regarded as the Father, which is the recognized center of each family unit, the Son, being He who is closest to the Father, and the Holy Ghost, being the Divinity of All.

A question often asked in relation to this Trinity is how each can be separate and yet one? Such is only a seeming paradox, as all is oneness in God.

JESUS THE CHRIST. In the Christian religion, Jesus the Christ is known as the Savior, the very center around which Christianity revolves. He is regarded as the Son of God and the Savior of Mankind.

Is Jesus truly the Son of God and divine? Unquestionably! But being divine is not his uniqueness, as all souls—through the spirit (The Holy Ghost)—are divine. What makes Him unique is in being a special advanced soul that returned for an incarnation in-body for a direct and distinct purpose—the bringing of salvation to mankind. Thus Jesus is, likewise, referred to as the SON OF MAN, since he was reborn in a human body.

Jesus is, thus, seen as a highly evolved soul who had obtained complete oneness with God (as the Bible refers to God and Christ as One and yet being somehow separate), on a special mission. There are miracles abounding about His birth, life, and death that mark Him clearly to all mankind, and places emphasis upon His purpose.

The mission of Christ was to show the way to God to all men

(as living souls in bodies) ; a way of living that leads to the growth of the spirit, the mastering of evil, the most rapid way of leaving the hell existence and of achieving the heaven state and oneness with God, as He, Himself, had achieved. He points the way, and all who will may follow.

Every so often in the history of man, in different times and different countries, such a "Wayshower" as Jesus the Christ (very possibly it may well be the same advanced soul) appears, each time in a different body incarnation, to direct mankind on the way of salvation.

SALVATION. This is a subject of special importance to the Christian. Other religions do not express it in the same manner. As a Christian, the way to the salvation of one's soul is the acceptance of Christ as one's personal Savior, which is another way of saying to *personally* follow the pathway to God which Christ spreads before one. Man cannot save himself, for salvation is not something earned. It is a gift; it is the heritage and right of every soul. But, it can only be achieved by following the way of Christ (accepting Christ and His way) for the upward evolution of the soul to the obtainment of oneness with God.

CHRISTIANITY VS. REINCARNATION. This is a subject that has been spoken of frequently in this book, since belief in reincarnation plays an important role in oriental religions, but Christians, in general, do not accept it. Christian doctrine presents a concept of the soul "sleeping" following death, until such time as it is called forth to stand in judgment before God, to be judged either worthy to live with God (in Heaven) or without God (in Hell). If the student will but penetrate to the heart of the true meaning here, it will be seen that in actuality such is but a means of expressing the soul-growth principle in a manner more understandable to occidental people than is the all-encompassing oriental one of reincarnation.

To explain a little, the concept of "sleeping" is obviously symbolic. The "sleeping" of the soul refers to its in-body experiences in rpeated incarnations, its "judgement before God" being the determining of its state of evolution and stature—whether it shows an advancement worthy of oneness with God (in Heaven), or assignment to further incarnations of development until such time as it is deemed worthy to enter the Kingdom of Heaven.

Naturally there are many religious differences on basic themes between the oriental religions and Christianity, as great as the differences between the peoples to whom they have meaning. They are all there to be studied, however Christians frequently tend to shy away from a study of other religions, using the excuse that they are too mystical. Actually, all religions are mystical and, in point of fact, Christianity is among the most mystical of all.

PRAYER. The Trinity in creation is surprisingly universal. God is regarded in trinity as the Father, the Son, and the Holy Ghost. Man is regarded in trinity as body, soul, and spirit. Mind is regarded in trinity as conscious, subconscious, and superconscious.

Prayer is a way of "talking" to the mind, and through the mind to God. To understand the action of prayer, it is well that we understand the action of mind functioning, in a way that will be instantly understandable to the western audience.

William Henry Mikesell, in his book, *Mental Hygiene,* states that there are five levels of conduct within us from which all behavior springs: instinct, reflex, habit, conscious thought, and the subconscious.

The first level, that of instinct, is located in the visceral region of the body where the impulses that drive us are felt. The midsection is the seat of the emotions; it is here where we feel most strongly. Even ambitions that lure to drive one to an enticing future are felt in the torso.

The second level, that of reflex, is controlled by both the spinal cord and the lower brain. Within its scope are the numerous reflexes with which we are all familiar, such as blinking our eyes, dodging from danger, reaching with the hands to explore, and many others.

The third level, that of habit behavior, probably located in the lower brain, works mechanically, as the reflex system does, but permeates the whole field of human endeavor.

The fourth level, that of conscious thought, is the crowning achievement of human performance. It is designed to work through, and control, the lower levels of response and to stand as the progressive and civilizing force of mankind.

The fifth level, that of the subconscious, is that part of us which permeates all of the four levels of conduct listed above. An impulse may have a subconscious origin. A reflex is generally subconscious. Habit, in its last stages, is controlled subconsciously. Conscious thought, itself, may be colored by subconscious control; much of discomforting behavior has its source in automatic functionings which strike their injurious shafts into the conscious phase of mind.

Since mind is one continuous whole there is obviously an interrelation, and that which is stored away in subconsciousness is bound to affect our reactions to that which is immediately in consciousness. After all, we are the sum total of our thoughts.

Within the subconscious—away from the field of conscious attention—are those automatic functions of the body such as heart action, digestion, etc., the control over which we normally expect to exert little or no influence. But even these, while they cannot be brought under complete voluntary control, can, to a surprising extent, be affected through the powerful action of suggestion, and by the methods of yoga.

Suggestion has been defined as the subconscious realization of an idea. Prayer is a way of implanting suggestions in the mind. And beyond the field of the psychologist, there is another phase of mind, the third in the trinity, the superconsciousness. This is the insight (mind-phase) of the soul that reaches directly through to God. This is the phase of mind that makes man immortal. Prayer may be thus seen to perform a dual function: the psychological effect of implanting ideas in the mind that subconsciously go into effect, and the function of providing a means of "talking" with God.

Prayers, in general, are thoughts of a profound nature, presented to the inner-mind in great sincerity, that either express thanks for "gifts" received or else ask for desired occurrences. As such, prayer functions by psychologically assisting and bolstering the individual in the achievement of his pattern of physical living, and, simultaneously, bringing his inner-self (the soul) into its intimate relationship (communion) with God. In practice, the mechanism of prayer commences on the conscious level, passes through into the subconscious, and proceeds into the superconsciousness in direct rapport with God.

As these viewpoints carry the oriental slant, I am certain that many western people will disagree with these "answers" on aspects of their favorite religion. Such is natural and as it should be. But the mark of maturity and growth is to study both sides of every question.

ON THE END OF THE JOURNEY.

As I quoted in Chapter Fourteen of this book, dealing with the art of meditation, the wise men of the East say, "The soul of the child and the soul of the sage are the same." They differ only in maturity, for a soul may be of any age—young or old.

I shall never look upon my fellow men in quite the same way as I did before this journey, for now I see their outward, physical countenance entirely as though it were but a suit of clothes being worn by the real person within. And children, how they have changed. Some tiny tots are obviously "old souls," while a person of venerable years can be a "young soul" indeed. It is remarkable how this truth has crept into our own colloquialisms, as the expression "he or she is an old soul" is frequently used as part of our language. From this time forward, look upon your fellow men in this light, and you will unquestionably note the status of the soul that stands before you, be it a young soul, a gradually maturing soul, or an old soul.

Magnificent oriental temples of worship testify to the oneness of man and the universality of his search for God and the true nature of his being.

We have completed our journey in the search of great religious mysteries of the Orient. It is no longer a journey into the unknown, for the illumination of truth has lighted the way. Man—from the earliest dawn of prehistory to the infinite reaches of the future—will always worship God, for he is instinctively aware of His being, and reaches ever toward that which is his heritage and to which he is perpetually ascending.

But the journey is never actually over; when the "door" opens, as it must for every man, step through with confidence with a wondrous realization of the amazing adventures that lie ahead in never-ending fascination.

"Eternal Father, help us to know
That we are in a house
Where the broadest tolerance
Has a right to be . . .
Where the least discordant word
Shall not be uttered . . .
Where all they who are here gathered
Recognize their duty to love one another
As brothers and sisters
In order to follow the unique plan of Thee,
The Creator . . . The Universal Conscience . . .
Father of All
To whatever race we belong,
From whatever country we come.
                    Amen"
From *The Master Way*
Great White Brotherhood of Caodai

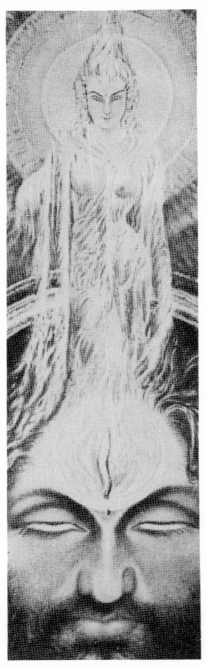

A rare East Indian print showing "The Flame Within," symbolic of the soul and man's immortality.

Index